Almanazor and Almahide by John Dryden

Or, The Conquest of Granada

A TRAGEDY.

THE SECOND PART.

—Stimulos dedit æmula virtus.
LUCAN.

John Dryden was born on August 9th, 1631 in the village rectory of Aldwincle near Thrapston in Northamptonshire. As a boy Dryden lived in the nearby village of Titchmarsh, Northamptonshire. In 1644 he was sent to Westminster School as a King's Scholar.

Dryden obtained his BA in 1654, graduating top of the list for Trinity College, Cambridge that year.

Returning to London during The Protectorate, Dryden now obtained work with Cromwell's Secretary of State, John Thurloe.

At Cromwell's funeral on 23 November 1658 Dryden was in the company of the Puritan poets John Milton and Andrew Marvell. The setting was to be a sea change in English history. From Republic to Monarchy and from one set of lauded poets to what would soon become the Age of Dryden.

The start began later that year when Dryden published the first of his great poems, Heroic Stanzas (1658), a eulogy on Cromwell's death.

With the Restoration of the Monarchy in 1660 Dryden celebrated in verse with Astraea Redux, an authentic royalist panegyric.

With the re-opening of the theatres after the Puritan ban, Dryden began to also write plays. His first play, The Wild Gallant, appeared in 1663 but was not successful. From 1668 on he was contracted to produce three plays a year for the King's Company, in which he became a shareholder. During the 1660s and '70s, theatrical writing was his main source of income.

In 1667, he published Annus Mirabilis, a lengthy historical poem which described the English defeat of the Dutch naval fleet and the Great Fire of London in 1666. It established him as the pre-eminent poet of his generation, and was crucial in his attaining the posts of Poet Laureate (1668) and then historiographer royal (1670).

This was truly the Age of Dryden, he was the foremost English Literary figure in Poetry, Plays, translations and other forms.

In 1694 he began work on what would be his most ambitious and defining work as translator, The Works of Virgil (1697), which was published by subscription. It was a national event.

John Dryden died on May 12th, 1700, and was initially buried in St. Anne's cemetery in Soho, before being exhumed and reburied in Westminster Abbey ten days later.

Index of Contents

DRAMATIS PERSONÆ

MAHOMET BOABDELIN, the last king of Granada.
Prince ABDALLA, his brother.
ABDELMELECH, chief of the Abencerrages.
ZULEMA, chief of the Zegrys.
ABENAMAR, an old Abencerrago.
SELIN, an old Zegry.
OZMYN, a brave young Abencerrago, son to Abenamar.
HAMET, brother to Zulema, a Zegry.
GOMEL, a Zegry.

ALMANZOR.
FERDINAND, king of Spain.
Duke of ARCOS, his General.
Don ALONZO D'AGUILAR, a Spanish Captain.

ALMAHIDE, Queen of Granada.
LYNDARAXA, Sister of ZULEMA, a Zegry Lady.
BENZAYDA, Daughter to SELIN.
ESPERANZA, Slave to the Queen.
HALYMA, Slave to LYNDARAXA.
ISABELLA, Queen of Spain.

Messengers, Guards, Attendants, Men, and Women.

PROLOGUE

TO THE SECOND PART

They, who write ill, and they, who ne'er durst write,
Turn critics, out of mere revenge and spite:
A playhouse gives them fame; and up there starts,
From a mean fifth-rate wit, a man of parts.
(So common faces on the stage appear;
We take them in, and they turn beauties here.)
Our author fears those critics as his fate;
And those he fears, by consequence must hate,
For they the traffic of all wit invade,
As scriveners draw away the bankers' trade.
Howe'er, the poet's safe enough to day,
They cannot censure an unfinished play.
But, as when vizard-mask appears in pit,
Straight every man, who thinks himself a wit,
Perks up, and, managing his comb with grace,
With his white wig sets off his nut-brown face;
That done, bears up to th' prize, and views each limb,
To know her by her rigging and her trim;
Then, the whole noise of fops to wagers go,—
"Pox on her, 'tmust be she;" and—"damme, no!"—
Just, so, I prophesy, these wits to-day
Will blindly guess at our imperfect play.
With what new plots our Second Part is filled,
Who must be kept alive, and who be killed.
And as those vizard-masks maintain that fashion,
To soothe and tickle sweet imagination;
So our dull poet keeps you on with masking,

To make you think there's something worth your asking.
But, when 'tis shown, that, which does now delight you,
Will prove a dowdy, with a face to fright you.

ALMANZOR AND ALMAHIDE,

OR, THE CONQUEST OF GRANADA.

THE SECOND PART.

ACT I

SCENE I.—A Camp.

Enter **KING FERDINAND, QUEEN ISABELLA, ALONZO D'AGUILAR; ATTENDANTS, MEN** and **WOMEN.**

KING FERDINAND
At length the time is come, when Spain shall be
From the long yoke of Moorish tyrants free.
All causes seem to second our design,
And heaven and earth in their destruction join.
When empire in its childhood first appears,
A watchful fate o'ersees its tender years;
Till, grown more strong, it thrusts and stretches out,
And elbows all the kingdoms round about:
The place thus made for its first breathing free,
It moves again for ease and luxury;
Till, swelling by degrees, it has possessed
The greater space, and now crowds up the rest;
When, from behind, there starts some petty state,
And pushes on its now unwieldy fate;
Then down the precipice of time it goes,
And sinks in minutes, which in ages rose.

QUEEN ISABELLA
Should bold Columbus in his search succeed,
And find those beds in which bright metals breed;
Tracing the sun, who seems to steal away,
That, miser-like, he might alone survey
The wealth which he in western mines did lay,—
Not all that shining ore could give my heart
The joy, this conquered kingdom will impart;
Which; rescued from these misbelievers' hands,
Shall now, at once, shake off its double bands:
At once to freedom and true faith restored,

Its old religion and its ancient lord.

KING FERDINAND
By that assault which last we made, I find,
Their courage is with their success declined:
Almanzor's absence now they dearly buy,
Whose conduct crowned their arms with victory.

ALONZO D'AGUILAR
Their king himself did their last sally guide;
I saw him, glistering in his armour, ride
To break a lance in honour of his bride:
But other thoughts now fill his anxious breast;
Care of his crown his love has dispossest.

[To them **ABDALLA**.

QUEEN ISABELLA
But see, the brother of the Moorish king:
He seems some news of great import to bring.

KING FERDINAND
He brings a spacious title to our side:
Those, who would conquer, must their foes divide.

ABDALLA
Since to my exile you have pity shown,
And given me courage yet to hope a throne;
While you without our common foes subdue,
I am not wanting to myself or you;
But have, within, a faction still alive,
Strong to assist, and secret to contrive,
And watching each occasion to foment
The people's fears into a discontent;
Which, from Almanzor's loss, before were great,
And now are doubled by their late defeat:
These letters from their chiefs the news assures.

[Gives letters to the **KING**.

KING FERDINAND
Be mine the honour, but the profit yours.

[To them the **DUKE OF ARCOS**, with **OZMYN** and **BENZAYDA**, Prisoners.

KING FERDINAND
That tertia of Italians did you guide,
To take their post upon the river side?

DUKE OF ARCOS

All are according to your orders placed:
My chearful soldiers their intrenchments haste;
The Murcian foot hath ta'en the upper ground,
And now the city is beleaguered round.

KING FERDINAND

Why is not then their leader here again?

DUKE OF ARCOS

The master of Alcantara is slain;
But he, who slew him, here before you stands:
It is that Moor whom you behold in bands.

KING FERDINAND

A braver man I had not in my host;
His murderer shall not long his conquest boast:
But, Duke of Arcos, say, how was he slain?

DUKE OF ARCOS

Our soldiers marched together on the plain;
We two rode on, and left them far behind,
Till, coming where we found the valley wind,
We saw these Moors; who, swiftly as they could,
Ran on to gain the covert of a wood.
This we observed; and, having crossed their way,
The lady, out of breath, was forced to stay:
The man then stood, and straight his faulchion drew;
Then told us, we in vain did those pursue,
Whom their ill fortune to despair did drive,
And yet, whom we should never take alive.
Neglecting this, the master straight spurred on;
But the active Moor his horse's shock did shun,
And, ere his rider from his reach could go,
Finished the combat with one deadly blow.
I, to revenge my friend, prepared to fight;
But now our foremost men were come in sight,
Who soon would have dispatched him on the place,
Had I not saved him from a death so base,
And brought him to attend your royal doom.

KING FERDINAND

A manly face, and in his age's bloom;
But, to content the soldiers, he must die:
Go, see him executed instantly.

QUEEN ISABELLA

Stay; I would learn his name before he go:
You, Prince Abdalla, may the prisoner know.

ABDALLA

Ozmyn's his name, and he deserves his fate;
His father heads the faction which I hate:
But much I wonder, that with him I see
The daughter of his mortal enemy.

BENZAYDA

'Tis true, by Ozmyn's sword my brother fell;
But 'twas a death he merited too well.
I know a sister should excuse his fault;
But you know too, that Ozmyn's death he sought,

ABDALLA

Our prophet has declared, by the event,
That Ozmyn is reserved for punishment;
For, when he thought his guilt from danger clear,
He, by new crimes, is brought to suffer here.

BENZAYDA

In love, or pity, if a crime you find,
We two have sinned above all human kind.

OZMYN

Heaven in my punishment has done a grace;
I could not suffer, in a better place:
That I should die by Christians it thought good,
To save your father's guilt, who sought my blood. [To her.

BENZAYDA

Fate aims so many blows to make us fall,
That 'tis in vain to think to ward them all:
And, where misfortunes great and many are,
Life grows a burden, and not worth our care.

OZMYN

I cast it from me, like a garment torn,
Ragged, and too indecent to be worn:
Besides, there is contagion in my fate, [To **BENZAYDA**.
It makes your life too much unfortunate.—
But, since her faults are not allied to mine,
In her protection let your favour shine.
To you, great queen, I make this last request,
(Since pity dwells in every royal breast)
Safe, in your care, her life and honour be:
It is a dying lover's legacy.

BENZAYDA

Cease, Ozmyn, cease so vain a suit to move;
I did not give you on those terms my love.
Leave me the care of me; for, when you go,
My love will soon instruct me what to do.

QUEEN ISABELLA

Permit me, sir, these lovers' doom to give:
My sentence is, they shall together live.
The courts of kings
To all distressed should sanctuaries be,
But most to lovers in adversity.
Castile and Arragon,
Which long against each other war did move,
My plighted lord and I have joined by love;
And, if to add this conquest heaven thinks good,
I would not have it stained with lovers' blood.

KING FERDINAND

Whatever Isabella shall command
Shall always be a law to Ferdinand.

BENZAYDA

The frowns of fate we will no longer fear.
Ill fate, great queen, can never find us here.

QUEEN ISABELLA

Your thanks some other time I will receive:
Henceforward safe in my protection live.
Granada is for noble loves renowned:
Her best defence is in her lovers found.
Love's an heroic passion, which can find
No room in any base degenerate mind:
It kindles all the soul with honour's fire,
To make the lover worthy his desire.
Against such heroes I success should fear,
Had we not too an host of lovers here.
An army, of bright beauties come with me;
Each lady shall her servant's actions see:
The fair and brave on each side shall contest;
And they shall overcome, who love the best.

[Exeunt.

SCENE II.—The Alhambra.

Enter **ZULEMA**.

ZULEMA
True, they have pardoned me; but do they know
What folly 'tis to trust a pardoned foe?
A blush remains in a forgiven face:
It wears the silent tokens of disgrace.
Forgiveness to the injured does belong;
But they ne'er pardon, who have done the wrong.
My hopeful fortunes lost! and, what's above
All I can name or think, my ruined love!
Feigned honesty shall work me into trust,
And seeming penitence conceal my lust.
Let heaven's great eye of Providence now take
One day of rest, and ever after wake.

[Enter **BOABDELIN**, **ABENAMAR**, and **GUARDS**.

BOABDELIN
Losses on losses! as if heaven decreed
Almanzor's valour should alone succeed.

ABENAMAR
Each sally we have made, since he is gone,
Serves but to pull our speedy ruin on.

BOABDELIN
Of all mankind, the heaviest fate he bears,
Who the last crown of sinking empire wears.
No kindly planet of his birth took care:
Heaven's outcast, and the dross of every star!

[A tumultuous noise within.

[Enter **ABDELMELECH**.

What new misfortunes do these cries presage?

ABDELMELECH
They are the effects of the mad people's rage.
All in despair tumultuously they swarm:
The fairest streets already take the alarm;
The needy creep from cellars under ground;
To them new cries from tops of garrets sound;
The aged from the chimneys seek the cold;
And wives from windows helpless infants hold.

BOABDELIN

See what the many-headed beast demands.—

[Exit **ABDELMELECH**.

Cursed is that king, whose's honour's in their hands.
In senates, either they too slowly grant,
Or saucily refuse to aid my want;
And, when their thrift has ruined me in war,
They call their insolence my want of care.

ABENAMAR

Cursed be their leaders, who that rage foment,
And veil, with public good, their discontent:
They keep the people's purses in their hands,
And hector kings to grant their wild demands;
But to each lure, a court throws out, descend,
And prey on those they promised to defend.

ZULEMA

Those kings, who to their wild demands consent,
Teach others the same way to discontent.
Freedom in subjects is not, nor can be;
But still, to please them, we must call them free.
Propriety, which they their idol make,
Or law, or law's interpreters, can shake.

ABENAMAR

The name of commonwealth is popular;
But there the people their own tyrants are.

BOABDELIN

But kings, who rule with limited command,
Have players' sceptres put into their hand.
Power has no balance, one side still weighs down,
And either hoists the commonwealth or crown;
And those, who think to set the scale more right,
By various turnings but disturb the weight.

ABENAMAR

While people tug for freedom, kings for power,
Both sink beneath some foreign conqueror:
Then subjects find too late they were unjust,
And want that power of kings, they durst not trust.

[To them **ABDELMELECH**.

ABDELMELECH

The tumult now is high, and dangerous grown:
The people talk of rendering up the town;
And swear that they will force the king's consent.

BOABDELIN
What counsel can this rising storm prevent?

ABDELMELECH
Their fright to no persuasions will give ear:
There's a deaf madness in a people's fear.

[Enter a **MESSENGER**.

MESSENGER
Their fury now a middle course does take;
To yield the town, or call Almanzor back.

BOABDELIN
I'll rather call my death.—
Go and bring up my guards to my defence:
I'll punish this outrageous insolence.

ABENAMAR
Since blind opinion does their reason sway,
You must submit to cure them their own way.
You to their fancies physic must apply;
Give them that chief on whom they most rely.
Under Almanzor prosperously they fought;
Almanzor, therefore, must with prayers be brought.

[Enter a **SECOND MESSENGER**.

2ND MESSENGER
Haste all you can their fury to assuage:
You are not safe from their rebellious rage.

[Enter a **THIRD MESSENGER**.

3RD MESSENGER
This minute, if you grant not their desire,
They'll seize your person, and your palace fire.

ABDELMELECH
Your danger, sir, admits of no delay.

BOABDELIN
In tumults people reign, and kings obey.—
Go and appease them with the vow I make,

That they shall have their loved Almanzor back.

[Exit **ABDELMELECH**

Almanzor has the ascendant o'er my fate;
I'm forced to stoop to one I fear and hate:
Disgraced, distressed, in exile, and alone,
He's greater than a monarch on his throne:
Without a realm, a royalty he gains;
Kings are the subjects over whom he reigns.

[A shout of acclamations within.

ABENAMAR
These shouts proclaim the people satisfied.

BOABDELIN
We for another tempest must provide.
To promise his return as I was loth,
So I want power now to perform my oath.
Ere this, for Afric he is sailed from Spain.

ABENAMAR
The adverse winds his passage yet detain;
I heard, last night, his equipage did stay
At a small village, short of Malaga.

BOABDELIN
Abenamar, this evening thither haste;
Desire him to forget his usage past:
Use all your rhetoric, promise, flatter, pray.

To them **ALMAHIDE**, attended.

ABENAMAR
Good fortune shows you yet a surer way:
Nor prayers nor promises his mind will move;
'Tis inaccessible to all, but love.

BOABDELIN
Oh, thou hast roused a thought within my breast,
That will for ever rob me of my rest.
Ah jealousy, how cruel is thy sting!
I, in Almanzor, a loved rival bring!
And now, I think, it is an equal strife,
If I my crown should hazard, or my wife.
Where, marriage, is thy cure, which husbands boast,
That in possession their desire is lost?

Or why have I alone that wretched taste,
Which, gorged and glutted, does with hunger last?
Custom and duty cannot set me free,
Even sin itself has not a charm for me.
Of married lovers I am sure the first,
And nothing but a king could be so curst.

ALMANZOR
What sadness sits upon your royal heart?
Have you a grief, and must not I have part?
All creatures else a time of love possess;
Man only clogs with cares his happiness:
And, while he should enjoy his part of bliss,
With thoughts of what may be, destroys what is.

BOABDELIN
You guess aright; I am oppressed with grief,
And 'tis from you that I must seek relief. [To the **COMPANY**]
Leave us; to sorrow there's a reverence due:
Sad kings, like suns eclipsed, withdraw from view.

[The **ATTENDANTS** go off, and chairs are set for the **KING** and **QUEEN**.

ALMANZOR
So, two kind turtles, when a storm is nigh,
Look up, and see it gathering in the sky:
Each calls his mate, to shelter in the groves,
Leaving, in murmur, their unfinished loves:
Perched on some drooping branch, they sit alone,
And coo, and hearken to each other's moan.

BOABDELIN
Since, Almahide, you seem so kind a wife,

[Taking her by the hand.

What would you do to save a husband's life?

ALMANZOR
When fate calls on that hard necessity,
I'll suffer death, rather than you shall die.

BOABDELIN
Suppose your country should in danger be;
What would you undertake to set it free?

ALMANZOR
It were too little to resign my breath.

My own free hand should give me nobler death.

BOABDELIN
That hand, which would so much for glory do,
Must yet do more; for it must kill me too.
You must kill me, for that dear country's sake;
Or, what's all one, must call Almanzor back.

ALMANZOR
I see to what your speech you now direct;
Either my love or virtue you suspect.
But know, that, when my person I resigned,
I was too noble not to give my mind.
No more the shadow of Almanzor fear;
I have no room, but for your image, here.

BOABDELIN
This, Almahide, would make me cease to mourn,
Were that Almanzor never to return:
But now my fearful people mutiny;
Their clamours call Almanzor back, not I.
Their safety, through my ruin, I pursue;
He must return, and must be brought by you.

ALMANZOR
That hour, when I my faith to you did plight,
I banished him for ever from my sight.
His banishment was to my virtue due;
Not that I feared him for myself, but you.
My honour had preserved me innocent:
But I would, your suspicion to prevent;
Which, since I see augmented in your mind,
I yet more reason for his exile find.

BOABDELIN
To your entreaties he will yield alone.
And on your doom depend my life and throne.
No longer, therefore, my desires withstand;
Or, if desires prevail not, my command.

ALMANZOR
In his return, too sadly I foresee
The effects of your returning jealousy.
But your command I prize above my life;
'Tis sacred to a subject and a wife:
If I have power, Almanzor shall return.

BOABDELIN

Cursed be that fatal hour when I was born!

[Letting go her hand, and starting up.

You love, you love him; and that love reveal,
By your too quick consent to his repeal.
My jealousy had but too just a ground;
And now you stab into my former wound.

ALMANZOR
This sudden change I do not understand.
Have you so soon forgot your own command?

BOABDELIN
Grant that I did the unjust injunction lay,
You should have loved me more than to obey.
I know you did this mutiny design;
But I'll your love-plot quickly countermine.
Let my crown go; he never shall return;
I, like a phoenix, in my nest will burn.

ALMANZOR
You please me well; that in one common fate
You wrap yourself, and me, and all your state.
Let us no more of proud Almanzor hear:
'Tis better once to die, than still to fear;
And better many times to die, than be
Obliged, past payment, to an enemy.

BOABDELIN
'Tis better; but you wives have still one way:
Whene'er your husbands are obliged, you pay.

ALMANZOR
Thou, heaven, who know'st it, judge my innocence!—
You, sir, deserve not I should make defence.
Yet, judge my virtue by that proof I gave,
When I submitted to be made your slave.

BOABDELIN
If I have been suspicious or unkind,
Forgive me; many cares distract my mind:
Love, and a crown!
Two such excuses no one man e'er had;
And each of them enough to make me mad:
But now my reason reassumes its throne,
And finds no safety when Almanzor's gone.
Send for him then; I'll be obliged, and sue;

'Tis a less evil than to part with you.
I leave you to your thoughts; but love me still!
Forgive my passion, and obey my will.

[Exit **BOABDELIN**.

[**ALMAHIDE** solus.

My jealous lord will soon to rage return;
That fire, his fear rakes up, does inward burn.
But heaven, which made me great, has chose for me,
I must the oblation for my people be.
I'll cherish honour, then, and life despise;
What is not pure, is not for sacrifice.
Yet for Almanzor I in secret mourn!
Can virtue, then, admit of his return?
Yes; for my love I will by virtue square;
My heart's not mine, but all my actions are.
I'll like Almanzor act; and dare to be
As haughty, and as wretched too, as he.
What will he think is in my message meant?
I scarcely understand my own intent:
But, silk-worm like, so long within have wrought,
That I am lost in my own web of thought.

[Exit **ALMAHIDE**.

ACT II

SCENE I.—A Wood

Enter **OZMYN** and **BENZAYDA**.

OZMYN
'Tis true, that our protection here has been
The effect of honour in the Spanish queen;
But, while I as a friend continue here,
I to my country must a foe appear.

BENZAYDA
Think not, my Ozmyn, that we here remain
As friends, but prisoners to the power of Spain.
Fortune dispenses with your country's right;
But you desert your honour in your flight.

OZMYN

I cannot leave you here, and go away;
My honour's glad of a pretence to stay.

[A noise within,—Follow, follow, follow!—

[Enter **SELIN**, his sword drawn, as pursued.

SELIN
I am pursued, and now am spent and done;
My limbs suffice me not with strength to run.
And, if I could, alas! what can I save?
A year, the dregs of life too, from the grave.

[Sits down on the ground.

Here will I sit, and here attend my fate,
With the same hoary majesty and state,
As Rome's old senate for the Gauls did wait.

BENZAYDA
It is my father; and he seems distressed.

OZMYN
My honour bids me succour the oppressed;
That life he sought, for his I'll freely give;
We'll die together, or together live.

BENZAYDA
I'll call more succour, since the camp is near,
And fly on all the wings of love and fear.

[Exit **BENZAYDA**.

[Enter **ABENAMAR**, and four or five **MOORS**. He looks and finds **SELIN**.

ABENAMAR
You've lived, and now behold your latest hour.

SELIN
I scorn your malice, and defy your power.
A speedy death is all I ask you now;
And that's a favour you may well allow.

OZMYN [shewing himself.]
Who gives you death, shall give it first to me;
Fate cannot separate our destiny.—[Knows his **FATHER**.
My father here! then heaven itself has laid
The snare, in which my virtue is betrayed.

ABENAMAR

Fortune, I thank thee! thou hast kindly done,
To bring me back that fugitive, my son;
In arms too? fighting for my enemy!—
I'll do a Roman justice,—thou shalt die!

OZMYN

I beg not you my forfeit life would save;
Yet add one minute to that breath you gave.
I disobeyed you, and deserve my fate;
But bury in my grave two houses' hate.
Let Selin live; and see your justice done
On me, while you revenge him for his son:
Your mutual malice in my death may cease,
And equal loss persuade you both to peace.

ABENAMAR

Yes, justice shall be done on him and thee.—
Haste and dispatch them both immediately. [To a **SOLDIER**.

OZMYN

If you have honour,—since you nature want,—
For your own sake my last petition grant;
And kill not a disarmed, defenceless foe,
Whose death your cruelty, or fear, will show.
My father cannot do an act so base:—
My father!—I mistake;—I meant, who was.

ABENAMAR

Go, then, dispatch him first who was my son!

OZMYN

Swear but to save his life, I'll yield my own.

ABENAMAR

Nor tears, nor prayers, thy life, or his, shall buy.

OZMYN

Then, sir, Benzayda's father shall not die!—

[Putting himself before **SELIN**.

And, since he'll want defence when I am gone,
I will, to save his life, defend my own.

ABENAMAR

This justice, parricides, like thee, should have!—

[ABENAMAR and his party attack them both. OZMYN parries his father's thrusts, and thrusts at the others.

[Enter BENZAYDA, with ABDALLA, the DUKE OF ARCOS, and SPANIARDS.

BENZAYDA
O, help my father! and my Ozmyn save!

ABDALLA
Villains, that death you have deserved is near!

OZMYN
Stay, prince! and know, I have a father here!—

[Stops ABDALLA'S hand.

I were that parricide, of whom he spoke,
Did not my piety prevent your stroke.

DUKE OF ARCOS (to ABENAMAR.
Depart, then, and thank heaven you had a son.

ABENAMAR
I am not with these shows of duty won.

OZMYN [to his FATHER]
Heaven knows, I would that life, you seek, resign;
But, while Benzayda lives, it is not mine.
Will you yet pardon my unwilling crime?

ABENAMAR
By no entreaties, by no length of time,
Will I be won; but, with my latest breath,
I'll curse thee here, and haunt thee after death.

[Exit ABENAMAR with his party.

OZMYN
Can you be merciful to that degree,

[Kneeling to SELIN.

As to forgive my father's faults in me?
Can you forgive
The death of him I slew in my defence,
And from the malice separate the offence?
I can no longer be your enemy:

In short, now kill me, sir, or pardon me.

[Offers him his sword.

In this your silence my hard fate appears.

SELIN
I'll answer you, when I can speak for tears.
But, till I can,
Imagine what must needs be brought to pass;

[Embraces him.

My heart's not made of marble, nor of brass.
Did I for you a cruel death prepare,
And have you, have you made my life your care!
There is a shame contracted by my faults,
Which hinders me to speak my secret thoughts.
And I will tell you—when the shame's removed—
You are not better by my daughter loved.—
Benzayda be yours.—I can no more.

OZMYN
Blessed be that breath which does my life restore!

[Embracing his knees.

BENZAYDA
I hear my father now; these words confess
That name, and that indulgent tenderness.

SELIN
Benzayda, I have been too much to blame;
But let your goodness expiate my shame:
You Ozmyn's virtue did in chains adore,
And part of me was just to him before.—
My son!—

OZMYN
My father!—

SELIN
Since by you I live,
I, for your sake, your family forgive.
Let your hard father still my life pursue,
I hate not him, but for his hate to you;
Even that hard father yet may one day be
By kindness vanquished, as you vanquished me;

Or, if my death can quench to you his rage,
Heaven makes good use of my remaining age.

ABDALLA
I grieve your joys are mingled with my cares;
But all take interest in their own affairs;
And, therefore, I must ask how mine proceed.

SELIN
They now are ripe, and but your presence need:
For Lyndaraxa, faithless as the wind,
Yet to your better fortunes will be kind;
For, hearing that the Christians own your cause,
From thence the assurance of a throne she draws.
And since Almanzor, whom she most did fear,
Is gone, she to no treaty will give ear;
But sent me her unkindness to excuse.

ABDALLA
You much surprise me with your pleasing news.

SELIN
But, sir, she hourly does the assault expect,
And must be lost if you her aid neglect:
For Abdelmelech loudly does declare,
He'll use the last extremities of war,
If she refuse the fortress to resign.

ABDALLA
The charge of hastening this relief be mine.

SELIN
This while I undertook, whether beset,
Or else by chance, Abenamar I met;
Who seemed, in haste, returning to the town.

ABDALLA
My love must in my diligence be shown.—
And [To **DUKE OF ARCOS**.] as my pledge of faith to Spain, this hour
I'll put the fortress in your master's power.

SELIN
An open way from hence to it there lies,
And we with ease may send in large supplies,
Free from the shot and sallies of the town.

DUKE OF ARCOS
Permit me, sir, to share in your renown;

First to my king I will impart the news,
And then draw out what succours we shall use.

[Exit **DUKE OF ARCOS**.

ABDALLA [Aside.]
Grant that she loves me not, at least I see
She loves not others, if she loves not me.—
'Tis pleasure, when we reap the fruit of pain:
'Tis only pride, to be beloved again.
How many are not loved, who think they are!
Yet all are willing to believe the fair;
And, though 'tis beauty's known and obvious cheat,
Yet man's self-love still favours the deceit.

[Exit **ABDALALLA**.

SELIN
Farewell, my children! equally so dear,
That I myself am to myself less near:
While I repeat the dangers of the war,
Your mutual safety be each other's care.
Your father, Ozmyn, till the war be done,
As much as honour will permit, I'll shun:
If by his sword I perish, let him know
It was, because I would not be his foe.

OZMYN
Goodness and virtue all your actions guide;
You only err in choosing of your side.
That party I, with honour, cannot take;
But can much less the care of you forsake:
I must not draw my sword against my prince,
But yet may hold a shield in your defence.
Benzayda, free from danger, here shall stay,
And for a father and a lover pray.

BENZAYDA
No, no! I gave not on those terms my heart,
That from my Ozmyn I should ever part:
That love I vowed, when you did death attend,
'Tis just that nothing but my death should end.
What merchant is it, who would stay behind,
His whole stock ventured to the waves and wind?
I'll pray for both, but both shall be in sight;
And heaven shall hear me pray, and see you fight.

SELIN

No longer, Ozmyn, combat a design,
Where so much love, and so much virtue join.

OZMYN [To **BENZAYDA**.]
Then conquer, and your conquest happy be,
Both to yourself, your father, and to me.—
With bended knees our freedom we'll demand
Of Isabel, and mighty Ferdinand:
Then while the paths of honour we pursue,
We'll interest heaven for us, in right of you.

[Exeunt.

SCENE II.—The Albayzyn.

An alarm within; then Soldiers running over the stage. Enter **ABDELMELECH**, victorious, with **SOLDIERS.**

ABDELMELECH
'Tis won, 'tis won! and Lyndaraxa, now,
Who scorned to treat, shall to a conquest bow.
To every sword I free commission give;
Fall on, my friends, and let no rebel live.
Spare only Lyndaraxa; let her be
In triumph led, to grace my victory.
Since by her falsehood she betrayed my love,
Great as that falsehood my revenge shall prove.—

[Enter **LYNDARAXA**, as frightened, attended by women.

Go, take the enchantress, bring her to me bound!

LYNDARAXA
Force needs not, where resistance is not found:
I come, myself, to offer you my hands;
And, of my own accord, invite your bands.
I wished to be my Abdelmelech's slave;
I did but wish,—and easy fortune gave.

ABDELMELECH
O, more than woman false!—but 'tis in vain.—
Can you ere hope to be believed again?
I'll sooner trust the hyæna, than your smile;
Or, than your tears, the weeping crocodile.
In war and love none should be twice deceived;
The fault is mine if you are now believed.

LYNDARAXA

Be overwise, then, and too late repent;
Your crime will carry its own punishment.
I am well pleased not to be justified;
I owe no satisfaction to your pride.
It will be more advantage to my fame,
To have it said, I never owned a flame.

ABDELMELECH

'Tis true, my pride has satisfied itself:
I have at length escaped the deadly shelf.
The excuses you prepare will be in vain,
Till I am fool enough to love again.

LYNDARAXA

Am I not loved?

ABDELMELECH

I must with shame avow,
I loved you once;—but do not love you now.

LYNDARAXA

Have I for this betrayed Abdalla's trust?
You are to me, as I to him, unjust. [Angrily.

ABDELMELECH

'Tis like you have done much for love of me,
Who kept the fortress of my enemy.

LYNDARAXA

'Tis true, I took the fortress from his hand;
But, since, have kept it in my own command.

ABDELMELECH

That act your foul ingratitude did show.

LYNDARAXA

You are the ungrateful, since 'twas kept for you.

ABDELMELECH

'Twas kept indeed; but not by your intent:
For all your kindness I may thank the event.
Blush, Lyndaraxa, for so gross a cheat:
'Twas kept for me,—when you refused to treat! [Ironically.

LYNDARAXA

Blind man! I knew the weakness of the place:
It was my plot to do your arms this grace.

Had not my care of your renown been great,
I loved enough to offer you to treat.
She, who is loved, must little lets create;
But you bold lovers are to force your fate.
This force, you used, my maiden blush will save;
You seemed to take, what secretly I gave.
I knew we must be conquered; but I knew
What confidence I might repose in you.
I knew, you were too grateful to expose
My friends, and soldiers, to be used like foes.

ABDELMELECH
Well, though I love you not, their lives shall be
Spared out of pity and humanity.—
Alferez, [To a **SOLDIER**] go, and let the slaughter cease.

[Exit the **ALFEREZ**.

LYNDARAXA
Then must I to your pity owe my peace?
Is that the tenderest term you can afford?
Time was, you would have used another word.

ABDELMELECH
Then, for your beauty I your soldiers spare:
For, though I do not love you, you are fair.

LYNDARAXA
That little beauty why did heaven impart,
To please your eyes, but not to move your heart!
I'll shroud this gorgon from all human view,
And own no beauty, since it charms not you!
Reverse your orders, and your sentence give;
My soldiers shall not from my beauty live.

ABDELMELECH
Then, from your friendship they their lives shall gain;
Tho' love be dead, yet friendship does remain.

LYNDARAXA
That friendship, which from withered love does shoot,
Like the faint herbage on a rock, wants root.
Love is a tender amity, refined:
Grafted on friendship it exalts the kind.
But when the graff no longer does remain,
The dull stock lives, but never bears again.

ABDELMELECH

Then, that my friendship may not doubtful prove,—
Fool that I am to tell you so!—I love.
You would extort this knowledge from my breast,
And tortured me so long that I confest.
Now I expect to suffer for my sin;
My monarchy must end, and yours begin.

LYNDARAXA
Confess not love, but spare yourself that shame,
And call your passion by some other name.
Call this assault, your malice, or your hate;
Love owns no acts so disproportionate.
Love never taught this insolence you shew,
To treat your mistress like a conquered foe.
Is this the obedience which my heart should move!
This usage looks more like a rape than love.

ABDELMELECH
What proof of duty would you I should give?

LYNDARAXA
'Tis grace enough to let my subjects live!
Let your rude soldiers keep possession still;
Spoil, rifle, pillage,—any thing but kill.
In short, sir, use your fortune as you please;
Secure my castle, and my person seize;
Let your true men my rebels hence remove;
I shall dream on, and think 'tis all your love!

ABDELMELECH
You know too well my weakness and your power:
Why did heaven make a fool a conqueror!
She was my slave, 'till she by me was shewn
How weak my force was, and how strong her own.
Now she has beat my power from every part,
Made her way open to my naked heart: [To a **SOLDIER**.
Go, strictly charge my soldiers to retreat:
Those countermand who are not entered yet.
On peril of your lives leave all things free.

[Exit **SOLDIER**.

Now, madam, love Abdalla more than me.
I only ask, in duty you would bring
The keys of our Albayzyn to the king:
I'll make your terms as gentle as you please.

[Trumpets sound a charge within, and **SOLDIERS** shout.

What shouts, and what new sounds of war are these?

LYNDARAXA
Fortune, I hope, has favoured my intent, [Aside.
Of gaining time, and welcome succours sent.

[Enter the **ALFEREZ**.

ALFEREZ
 All's lost, and you are fatally deceived:
The foe is entered, and the place relieved.
Scarce from the walls had I drawn off my men,
When, from their camp, the enemy rushed in,
And prince Abdalla entered first the gate.

ABDELMELECH
I am betrayed, and find it now too late.
When your proud soul to flatteries did descend, [To her.
I might have known it did some ill portend.
The weary seaman stormy weather fears,
When winds shift often, and no cause appears.
You by my bounty live—
Your brothers, too, were pardoned for my sake,
And this return your gratitude does make.

LYNDARAXA
My brothers best their own obligement know;
Without your charging me with what they owe.
But, since you think the obligement is so great,
I'll bring a friend to satisfy my debt.

[Looking behind.

ABDELMELECH
Thou shalt not triumph in thy base design;
Though not thy fort, thy person shall be mine.

[He goes to take her: She runs and cries out help.

[Enter **ABDALLA, DUKE OF ARCOS**, and **SPANIARDS. ABDELMELECH** retreats fighting, and is pursued by
the adverse party off the stage. The alarm within.

[Enter again **ABDALLA** and the **DUKE OF ARCOS**, with **LYNDARAXA**.

DUKE OF ARCOS
Bold Abdelmelech twice our Spaniards faced,
Though much out-numbered; and retreated last.

ABDALLA
Your beauty, as it moves no common fire, [To **LYNDARAXA**]
So it no common courage can inspire.
As he fought well, so had he prospered too,
If, madam, he, like me, had fought for you.

LYNDARAXA
Fortune, at last, has chosen with my eyes;
And, where I would have given it, placed the prize.
You see, sir, with what hardship I have kept
This precious gage, which in my hands you left.
But 'twas the love of you which made me fight,
And gave me courage to maintain your right.
Now, by experience, you my faith may find,
And are to thank me that I seemed unkind.
When your malicious fortune doomed your fall,
My care restrained you then from losing all;
Against your destiny I shut the gate,
And gathered up the shipwrecks of your fate;
I, like a friend, did even yourself withstand,
From throwing all upon a losing hand.

ABDALLA
My love makes all your acts unquestioned go,
And sets a sovereign stamp on all you do.
Your love I will believe with hood-winked eyes;—
In faith, much merit in much blindness lies.
But now, to make you great as you are fair,
The Spaniards an imperial crown prepare.

LYNDARAXA
That gift's more welcome, which with you I share.
Let us no time in fruitless courtship lose,
But sally out upon our frighted foes.
No ornaments of power so please my eyes,
As purple, which the blood of princes dies.

[Exeunt.

SCENE III.—The Alhambra.

BOABDELIN, ABENAMAR, ALMAHIDE, and **GUARDS,** &c. The **QUEEN** wearing a scarf.

ABENAMAR
My little journey has successful been,

The fierce Almanzor will obey the queen.
I found him, like Achilles on the shore,
Pensive, complaining much, but threatening more;
And, like that injured Greek, he heard our woes,
Which, while I told, a gloomy smile arose
From his bent brows: And still, the more he heard,
A more severe and sullen joy appeared.
But, when he knew we to despair were driven,
Betwixt his teeth he muttered thanks to heaven.

BOABDELIN
How I disdain this aid! which I must take,
Not for my own, but Almahide's sake.

ABENAMAR
But when he heard it was the queen who sent,
That her command repealed his banishment,
He took the summons with a greedy joy,
And asked me how she would his sword employ:
Then bid me say, her humblest slave would come,
From her fair mouth with joy to take his doom.

BOABDELIN
Oh that I had not sent you! though it cost
My crown! though I, and it, and all were lost!

ABENAMAR
While I, to bring this news, came on before,
I met with Selin—

BOABDELIN
I can hear no more.

[Enter **HAMET**.

HAMET
 Almanzor is already at the gate,
And throngs of people on his entrance wait.

BOABDELIN
Thy news does all my faculties surprise;
He bears two basilisks in those fierce eyes;
And that tame dæmon, which should guard my throne,
Shrinks at a genius greater than his own.

[Exit **BOABDELIN** with **ABENAMAR** and **GUARDS**.

[Enter **ALMANZOR**; seeing **ALMAHIDE** approach him, he speaks.

ALMANZOR

 So Venus moves, when to the Thunderer,
In smiles or tears, she would some suit prefer;
When with her cestus girt,
And drawn by doves, she cuts the liquid skies,
And kindles gentle fires where'er she flies:
To every eye a goddess is confest,
By all the heavenly nation she is blest,
And each with secret joy admits her to his breast.—
Madam your new commands I come to know,
If yet you can have any where I go.

[To her bowing.

If to the regions of the dead they be,
You take the speediest course to send by me.

ALMAHIDE

Heaven has not destined you so soon to rest:
Heroes must live to succour the distrest.

ALMANZOR

 To serve such beauty all mankind should live;
And, in our service, our reward you give.
But stay me not in torture, to behold
And ne'er enjoy. As from another's gold
The miser hastens, in his own defence,
And shuns the sight of tempting excellence;
So, having seen you once so killing fair,
A second sight were but to move despair.
I take my eyes from what too much would please,
As men in fevers famish their disease.

ALMAHIDE

No; you may find your cure an easier way,
If you are pleased to seek it,—in your stay.
All objects lose by too familiar view,
When that great charm is gone, of being new;
By often seeing me, you soon will find
Defects so many, in my face and mind,
That to be freed from love you need not doubt;
And, as you looked it in, you'll look it out.

ALMANZOR

 I rather, like weak armies, should retreat,
And so prevent my more entire defeat.
For your own sake in quiet let me go;

Press not too far on a despairing foe:
I may turn back, and armed against you move,
With all the furious train of hopeless love.

ALMAHIDE
Your honour cannot to ill thoughts give way,
And mine can run no hazard by your stay.

ALMANZOR
 Do you then think I can with patience see
That sovereign good possessed, and not by me?
No; I all day shall languish at the sight,
And rave on what I do not see all night;
My quick imagination will present
The scenes and images of your content.

ALMAHIDE
These are the day-dreams which wild fancy yields,
Empty as shadows are, that fly o'er fields.
Oh, whither would this boundless fancy move!
'Tis but the raging calenture of love.
Like a distracted passenger you stand,
And see, in seas, imaginary land,
Cool groves, and flowery meads; and while you think
To walk, plunge in, and wonder that you sink.

ALMANZOR
 Love's calenture too well I understand;
But sure your beauty is no fairy-land!
Of your own form a judge you cannot be;
For, glow-worm like, you shine, and do not see.

ALMAHIDE
Can you think this, and would you go away?

ALMANZOR
 What recompence attends me, if I stay?

ALMAHIDE
You know I am from recompence debarred,
But I will grant your merit a reward;
Your flame's too noble to deserve a cheat,
And I too plain to practise a deceit.
I no return of love can ever make,
But what I ask is for my husband's sake;
He, I confess, has been ungrateful too,
But he and I are ruined if you go;
Your virtue to the hardest proof I bring,—

Unbribed, preserve a mistress and a king.

ALMANZOR
I'll stop at nothing that appears so brave:
I'll do't, and now I no reward will have.
You've given my honour such an ample field,
That I may die, but that shall never yield.
Spite of myself I'll stay, fight, love, despair;
And I can do all this, because I dare.
Yet I may own one suit—
That scarf, which, since by you it has been borne,
Is blessed, like relicks which by saints were worn.

ALMAHIDE
Presents like this my virtue durst not make,
But that 'tis given you for my husband's sake.

[Gives the scarf.

ALMANZOR
This scarf to honourable rags I'll wear,
As conquering soldiers tattered ensigns bear;
But oh, how much my fortune I despise,
Which gives me conquest, while she love denies!

[Exeunt.

ACT III

SCENE I.—The Alhambra.

Enter **ALMAHIDE** and **ESPERANZA**.

ESPERANZA
Affected modesty has much of pride;
That scarf he begged, you could not have denied;
Nor does it shock the virtue of a wife,
When given that man, to whom you owe your life.

ALMAHIDE
Heaven knows, from all intent of ill 'twas free,
Yet it may feed my husband's jealousy;
And for that cause I wish it were not done.

[To them **BOABDELIN**, and walks apart.

See, where he comes, all pensive and alone;
A gloomy fury has o'erspread his face:
'Tis so! and all my fears are come to pass.

BOABDELIN
Marriage, thou curse of love, and snare of life, [Aside
That first debased a mistress to a wife!
Love, like a scene, at distance should appear,
But marriage views the gross-daubed landscape near.
Love's nauseous cure! thou cloyest whom thou should'st please;
And, when thou cur'st, then thou art the disease.
When hearts are loose, thy chain our bodies ties;
Love couples friends, but marriage enemies.
If love like mine continues after thee,
'Tis soon made sour, and turned by jealousy;
No sign of love in jealous men remains,
But that which sick men have of life—their pains.

ALMAHIDE
Has my dear lord some new affliction had?

[Walking to him.

Have I done any thing that makes him sad?

BOABDELIN
You! nothing: You! But let me walk alone.

ALMAHIDE
I will not leave you till the cause be known:
My knowledge of the ill may bring relief.

BOABDELIN
Thank ye; you never fail to cure my grief!
Trouble me not, my grief concerns not you.

ALMAHIDE
While I have life, I will your steps pursue.

BOABDELIN
I'm out of humour now; you must not stay.

ALMAHIDE
I fear it is that scarf I gave away.

BOABDELIN
No, 'tis not that; but speak of it no more:
Go hence! I am not what I was before.

ALMAHIDE
Then I will make you so; give me your hand!
Can you this pressing and these tears withstand?

BOABDELIN
Oh heaven, were she but mine, or mine alone!

[Sighing, and going off from her.

Ah, why are not the hearts of women known!
False women to new joys unseen can move;
There are no prints left in the paths of love,
All goods besides by public marks are known;
But what we most desire to keep, has none.

ALMAHIDE
Why will you in your breast your passion crowd,

[Approaching him.

Like unborn thunder rolling in a cloud?
Torment not your poor heart, but set it free,
And rather let its fury break on me.
I am not married to a god; I know,
Men must have passions, and can bear from you.
I fear the unlucky present I have made!

BOABDELIN
O power of guilt! how conscience can upbraid!
It forces her not only to reveal,
But to repeat what she would most conceal!

ALMAHIDE
Can such a toy, and given in public too—

BOABDELIN
False woman, you contrived it should be so.
That public gift in private was designed
The emblem of the love you meant to bind.
Hence from my sight, ungrateful as thou art!
And, when I can, I'll banish thee my heart.

[She weeps.

[To them **ALMANZOR** wearing the Scarf. He sees her weep.

ALMANZOR

What precious drops are those,
Which silently each other's track pursue,
Bright as young diamonds in their infant dew?
Your lustre you should free from tears maintain,
Like Egypt, rich without the help of rain.
Now cursed be he who gave this cause of grief;
And double cursed, who does not give relief!

ALMAHIDE
Our common fears, and public miseries,
Have drawn these tears from my afflicted eyes.

ALMANZOR
Madam, I cannot easily believe
It is for any public cause you grieve.
On your fair face the marks of sorrow lie;
But I read fury in your husband's eye:
And, in that passion, I too plainly find
That you're unhappy, and that he's unkind.

ALMAHIDE
Not new-made mothers greater love express
Than he, when with first looks their babes they bless;
Not Heaven is more to dying martyrs kind,
Nor guardian angels to their charge assigned.

BOABDELIN
O goodness counterfeited to the life!
O the well-acted virtue of a wife!
Would you with this my just suspicions blind?
You've given me great occasion to be kind!
The marks, too, of your spotless love appear;
Witness the badge of my dishonour there.

[Pointing to **ALMANZOR**'S scarf.

ALMANZOR
Unworthy owner of a gem so rare!
Heavens! why must he possess, and I despair?
Why is this miser doomed to all this store;
He, who has all, and yet believes he's poor?

ALMAHIDE [to **ALMANZOR**.]
You're much too bold, to blame a jealousy
So kind in him, and so desired by me.
The faith of wives would unrewarded prove,
Without those just observers of our love.
The greater care the higher passion shows;

We hold that clearest we most fear to lose.
Distrust in lovers is too warm a sun,
But yet 'tis night in love when that is gone;
And in those climes which most his scorching know,
He makes the noblest fruits and metals grow.

ALMANZOR
 Yes; there are mines of treasure in your breast,
Seen by that jealous sun, but not possest.
He, like a devil, among the blest above,
Can take no pleasure in your heaven of love.
Go, take her; and thy causeless fears remove; [To the **KING**.
Love her so well, that I with rage may die:
Dull husbands have no right to jealousy:
If that's allowed, it must in lovers be.

BOABDELIN
The succour, which thou bring'st me, makes thee bold:
But know, without thy aid, my crown I'll hold;
Or, if I cannot, I will fire the place,
Of a full city make a naked space.
Hence, then, and from a rival set me free!
I'll do, I'll suffer any thing but thee.

ALMANZOR
 I wonnot go; I'll not be forced away:
I came not for thy sake; nor do I stay.
It was the queen who for my aid did send;
And 'tis I only can the queen defend:
I, for her sake, thy sceptre will maintain;
And thou, by me, in spite of thee, shalt reign.

BOABDELIN
Had I but hope I could defend this place
Three days, thou should'st not live to my disgrace
So small a time;
Might I possess my Almahide alone,
I would live ages out ere they were gone.
I should not be of love or life bereft;
All should be spent before, and nothing left.

ALMAHIDE [to **BOABDELIN**]
As for your sake I for Almanzor sent,
So, when you please, he goes to banishment.
You shall, at last, my loyalty approve:
I will refuse no trial of my love.

BOABDELIN

How can I think you love me, while I see
That trophy of a rival's victory?
I'll tear it from his side.

ALMANZOR
 I'll hold it fast
As life, and when life's gone, I'll hold this last;
And if thou tak'st it after I am slain,
I'll send my ghost to fetch it back again.

ALMAHIDE
When I bestowed that scarf, I had not thought,
Or not considered it might be a fault;
But, since my lord's displeased that I should make
So small a present, I command it back.
Without delay the unlucky gift restore;
Or, from this minute, never see me more.

ALMANZOR
 The shock of such a curse I dare not stand:

[Pulling it off hastily, and presenting it to her.

Thus I obey your absolute command.

[She gives it to the **KING**.

Must he the spoils of scorn'd Almanzor wear?—
May Turnus' fate be thine, who dared to bear
The belt of murdered Pallas! from afar
Mayest thou be known, and be the mark of war!
Live, just to see it from thy shoulders torn
By common hands, and by some coward worn.

[An alarm within.

[Enter **ABDELMELECH, ZULEMA**, HAMET, **ABENAMAR**; their swords drawn.

ABDELMELECH
Is this a time for discord or for grief?
We perish, sir, without your quick relief.
I have been fooled, and am unfortunate;
The foes pursue their fortune and our fate.

ZULEMA
The rebels with the Spaniards are agreed.

BOABDELIN

Take breath; my guards shall to the fight succeed.

ABENAMAR [to **ALMANZOR**.]
Why stay you, sir? the conquering foe is near:
Give us their courage, and give them our fear.

HAMET
 Take arms, or we must perish in your sight.

ALMANZOR
 I care not: perish: for I will not fight,
I wonnot lift an arm in his defence:
And yet I wonnot stir one foot from hence.
I to your king's defence his town resign;
This only spot, whereon I stand, is mine.—
Madam, be safe, and lay aside your fear, [To the **QUEEN**
You are as in a magic circle here.

BOABDELIN
To our own valour our success we'll owe.
Haste, Hamet, with Abenamar to go;
You two draw up, with all the speed you may,
Our last reserves, and yet redeem the day.

[Exeunt **HAMET** and **ABENAMAR** one way, the **KING** the other, with **ABDELMELECH**, &c.

[Alarm within.

[Enter **ABDELMELECH**, his sword drawn.

ABDELMELECH
Granada is no more! the unhappy king
Venturing too far, ere we could succour bring,
Was by the duke of Arcos prisoner made,
And, past relief, is to the fort conveyed.

ALMANZOR
 Heaven, thou art just! go, now despise my aid.

ALMAHIDE
Unkind Almanzor, how am I betrayed!
Betrayed by him in whom I trusted most!
But I will ne'er outlive what I have lost.
Is this your succour, this your boasted love!
I will accuse you to the saints above!
Almanzor vowed he would for honour fight,
And lets my husband perish in my sight.

[Exeunt ALMAHIDE and ESPERANZA.

ALMANZOR
Oh, I have erred; but fury made me blind;
And, in her just reproach, my fault I find!
I promised even for him to fight, whom I—
But since he's loved by her, he must not die.
Thus, happy fortune comes to me in vain,
When I myself must ruin it again.

[To him ABENAMAR, HAMET, ABDELMELECH, ZULEMA, SOLDIERS.

ABENAMAR
The foe has entered the Vermillion towers;
And nothing but the Alhambra now is ours.

ALMANZOR
Even that's too much, except we may have more;
You lost it all to that last stake before.
Fate, now come back; thou canst not farther get;
The bounds of thy libration here are set.
Thou know'st this place,
And, like a clock wound up, strik'st here for me;
Now, Chance, assert thy own inconstancy,
And, Fortune, fight, that thou may'st Fortune be!—
They come: here, favoured by the narrow place,

[A noise within.

I can, with few, their gross battalion face.
By the dead wall, you, Abdelmelech, wind;
Then charge, and their retreat cut off behind.

[Exeunt.

[An alarm within.

[Enter ALMANZOR and his PARTY, with ABDALLA prisoner.

ALMANZOR
You were my friend: and to that name I owe [To ABDALLA.
The just regard, which you refused to show.
Your liberty I frankly would restore,
But honour now forbids me to do more.
Yet, sir, your freedom in your choice shall be,
When you command to set your brother free.

ABDALLA

The exchange, which you propose, with joy I take;
An offer easier than my hopes could make.
Your benefits revenge my crimes to you,
For I my shame in that bright mirror view.

ALMANZOR

 No more; you give me thanks you do not owe:
I have been faulty, and repent me now.
But, though our penitence a virtue be,
Mean souls alone repent in misery;
The brave own faults when good success is given,
For then they come on equal terms to heaven.

[Exeunt.

SCENE II.—The Albayzyn.

Enter **OZMYN** and **BENZAYDA**.

BENZAYDA

I see there's somewhat which you fear to tell;
Speak quickly, Ozmyn, is my father well?
Why cross you thus your arms, and shake your head?
Kill me at once, and tell me he is dead.

OZMYN

I know not more than you; but fear not less;
Twice sinking, twice I drew him from the press:
But the victorious foe pursued so fast,
That flying throngs divided us at last.
As seamen parting in a general wreck,
When first the loosening planks begin to crack;
Each catches one, and straight are far disjoined,
Some borne by tides, and others by the wind;
So, in this ruin, from each other rent,
With heaved-up hands we mutual farewells sent:
Methought his eyes, when just I lost his view,
Were looking blessings to be sent to you.

BENZAYDA

Blind queen of Chance, to lovers too severe,
Thou rulest mankind, but art a tyrant there!
Thy widest empire's in a lover's breast:
Like open seas, we seldom are at rest.
Upon thy coasts our wealth is daily cast;
And thou, like pirates, mak'st no peace to last.

[To them **LYNDARAXA, DUKE OF ARCOS**, and **GUARDS.**

DUKE OF ARCOS
We were surprised when least we did suspect,
And justly suffered by our own neglect.

LYNDARAXA
No; none but I have reason to complain!
So near a kingdom, yet 'tis lost again!
O, how unequally in me were joined
A creeping fortune, with a soaring mind!
O lottery of fate! where still the wise
Draw blanks of fortune, and the fools the prize!
These cross, ill-shuffled lots from heaven are sent,
Yet dull Religion teaches us content;
But when we ask it where the blessing dwells,
It points to pedant colleges, and cells;
There shows it rude, and in a homely dress,
And that proud Want mistakes for happiness.

[A trumpet within.

[Enter **ZULEMA**.

Brother! what strange adventure brought you here?

ZULEMA
The news I bring will yet more strange appear.
The little care you of my life did show,
Has of a brother justly made a foe;
And Abdelmelech who that life did save,
As justly has deserved that life he gave.

LYNDARAXA
Your business cools, while tediously it stays
On the low theme of Abdelmelech's praise.

ZULEMA
This I present from Prince Abdalla's hands.

[Delivers a letter, which she reads.

LYNDARAXA
He has proposed, (to free him from his bands)
That, with his brother, an exchange be made.

DUKE OF ARCOS

It proves the same design which we had laid.
Before the castle let a bar be set;
And when the captives on each side are met,
With equal numbers chosen for their guard,
Just at the time the passage is unbarred,
Let both at once advance, at once be free.

LYNDARAXA

The exchange I will myself in person see.

BENZAYDA

I fear to ask, yet would from doubt be freed,—
Is Selin captive, sir, or is he dead?

ZULEMA

I grieve to tell you what you needs must know,—
He is a prisoner to his greatest foe;
Kept with strong guards in the Alhambra tower;
Without the reach even of Almanzor's power.

OZMYN

With grief and shame I am at once opprest.

ZULEMA

You will be more, when I relate the rest.
To you I from Abenamar am sent, [To **OZMYN**.
And you alone can Selin's death prevent.
Give up yourself a prisoner in his stead;
Or, ere to-morrow's dawn, believe him dead.

BENZAYDA

Ere that appear, I shall expire with grief.

ZULEMA

Your action swift, your counsel must be brief.

LYNDARAXA

While for Abdalla's freedom we prepare,
You in each other's breast unload your care.

[Exeunt all but **OZMYN** and **BENZAYDA**.

BENZAYDA

My wishes contradictions must imply;
You must not go; and yet he must not die.
Your reason may, perhaps, the extremes unite;
But there's a mist of fate before my sight.

OZMYN

The two extremes too distant are, to close;
And human wit can no mid way propose.
My duty therefore shows the nearest way
To free your father, and my own obey.

BENZAYDA

Your father, whom, since yours, I grieve to blame,
Has lost, or quite forgot, a parent's name;
And, when at once possessed of him and you,
Instead of freeing one, will murder two.

OZMYN

Fear not my life; but suffer me to go:
What cannot only sons with parents do!
'Tis not my death my father does pursue;
He only would withdraw my love from you.

BENZAYDA

Now, Ozmyn, now your want of love I see;
For would you go, and hazard losing me?

OZMYN

I rather would ten thousand lives forsake;
Nor can you e'er believe the doubt you make.
This night I with a chosen band will go,
And, by surprise, will free him from the foe.

BENZAYDA

What foe! ah whither would your virtue fall!
It is your father whom the foe you call.
Darkness and rage will no distinction make,
And yours may perish for my father's sake.

OZMYN

Thus, when my weaker virtue goes astray.
Yours pulls it back, and guides me in the way:
I'll send him word, my being shall depend
On Selin's life, and with his death shall end.

BENZAYDA

'Tis that, indeed, would glut your father's rage:
Revenge on Ozmyn's youth, and Selin's age.

OZMYN

Whate'er I plot, like Sysiphus, in vain
I heave a stone, that tumbles down again.

BENZAYDA

This glorious work is then reserved for me:
He is my father, and I'll set him free.
These chains my father for my sake does wear:
I made the fault; and I the pains will bear.

OZMYN

Yes; you no doubt have merited these pains;
Those hands, those tender limbs, were made for chains!
Did I not love you, yet it were too base
To let a lady suffer in my place.
Those proofs of virtue you before did show,
I did admire; but I must envy now.
Your vast ambition leaves no fame for me,
But grasps at universal monarchy.

BENZAYDA

Yes, Ozmyn, I shall still this palm pursue;
I will not yield my glory even to you.
I'll break those bonds in which my father's tied,
Or, if I cannot break them, I'll divide.
What, though my limbs a woman's weakness show,
I have a soul as masculine as you;
And when these limbs want strength my chains to wear,
My mind shall teach my body how to bear.

[Exit **BENZAYDA.**

OZMYN

What I resolve, I must not let her know;
But honour has decreed she must not go.
What she resolves, I must prevent with care;
She shall not in my fame or danger share.
I'll give strict order to the guards which wait,
That, when she comes, she shall not pass the gate.
Fortune, at last, has run me out of breath;
I have no refuge but the arms of death:
To that dark sanctuary I will go;
She cannot reach me when I lie so low.

[Exit.

SCENE III.—The Albayzyn.

Enter, on one side, **ALMANZOR, ABDALLA, ABDELMELECH, ZULEMA, HAMET**. On the other side, the
DUKE OF ARCOS, BOABDELIN, LYNDARAXA, and their **PARTY**. After which the bars are opened; and at

the same time **BOABDELIN** and **ABDALLA** pass by each other, each to his Party; when **ABDALLA** is passed on the other side, the **DUKE OF ARCOS** approaches the bars, and calls to **ALMANZOR**.

DUKE OF ARCOS
The hatred of the brave with battles ends,
And foes, who fought for honour, then are friends.
I love thee, brave Almanzor, and am proud
To have one hour when love may be allowed.
This hand, in sign of that esteem, I plight;
We shall have angry hours enough to fight.

[Giving his hand.

ALMANZOR
 The man who dares, like you, in fields appear,
And meet my sword, shall be my mistress here.
If I am proud, 'tis only to my foes;
Rough but to such who virtue would oppose.
If I some fierceness from a father drew,
A mother's milk gives me some softness too.

DUKE OF ARCOS
Since first you took, and after set me free,
(Whether a sense of gratitude it be,
Or some more secret motion of my mind,
For which I want a name that's more than kind)
I shall be glad, by whate'er means I can,
To get the friendship of so brave a man;
And would your unavailing valour call,
From aiding those whom heaven has doomed to fall.
We owe you that respect,
Which to the gods of foes besieged was shown,
To call you out before we take your town.

ALMANZOR
 Those whom we love, we should esteem them too,
And not debauch that virtue which we woo.
Yet, though you give my honour just offence,
I'll take your kindness in the better sense;
And, since you for my safety seem to fear,
I, to return your bribe, should wish you here.
But, since I love you more than you do me,
In all events preserve your honour free;
For that's your own, though not your destiny.

DUKE OF ARCOS
Were you obliged in honour by a trust,
I should not think my own proposals just;

But since you fight for an unthankful king,
What loss of fame can change of parties bring?

ALMANZOR
 It will, and may with justice too be thought,
That some advantage in that change I sought.
And though I twice have changed for wrongs received,
That it was done for profit none believed.
The king's ingratitude I knew before;
So that can be no cause of changing more.
If now I stand, when no reward can be,
'Twill show the fault before was not in me.

DUKE OF ARCOS
Yet there is a reward to valour due,
And such it is as may be sought by you;
That beauteous queen, whom you can never gain,
While you secure her husband's life and reign.

ALMANZOR
 Then be it so; let me have no return

[Here **LYNDARAXA** comes near, and hears them.

From him but hatred, and from her but scorn.
There is this comfort in a noble fate,
That I deserve to be more fortunate.
You have my last resolve; and now, farewell:
My boding heart some mischief does foretell;
But what it is, heaven will not let me know.
I'm sad to death, that I must be your foe.

DUKE OF ARCOS
Heaven, when we meet, if fatal it must be
To one, spare him, and cast the lot on me.

[They retire.

LYNDARAXA
Ah, what a noble conquest were this heart!
I am resolved I'll try my utmost art:
In gaining him, I gain that fortune too,
Which he has wedded, and which I but woo.
I'll try each secret passage to his mind,
And love's soft bands about his heart-strings wind.
Not his vowed constancy shall 'scape my snare;
While he without resistance does prepare,
I'll melt into him ere his love's aware.

[She makes a gesture of invitation to **ALMANZOR**, who returns again.

LYNDARAXA
You see, sir, to how strange a remedy
A persecuted maid is forced to fly:
Who, much distressed, yet scarce has confidence
To make your noble pity her defence.

ALMANZOR
 Beauty, like yours, can no protection need;
Or, if it sues, is certain to succeed.
To whate'er service you ordain my hand,
Name your request, and call it your command.

LYNDARAXA
You cannot, sir, but know, that my ill fate
Has made me loved with all the effects of hate:
One lover would, by force, my person gain;
Which one, as guilty, would by force detain.
Rash Abdelmelech's love I cannot prize,
And fond Abdalla's passion I despise.
As you are brave, so you are prudent too;
Advise a wretched woman what to do.

ALMANZOR
 Have courage, fair one, put your trust in me;
You shall, at least, from those you hate, be free.
Resign your castle to the king's command,
And leave your love concernments in my hand.

LYNDARAXA
The king, like them, is fierce, and faithless too;
How can I trust him who has injured you?
Keep for yourself, (and you can grant no less)
What you alone are worthy to possess.
Enter, brave sir; for, when you speak the word,
These gates will open of their own accord;
The genius of the place its lord will meet,
And bend its tow'ry forehead to your feet.
That little citadel, which now you see,
Shall, then, the head of conquered nations be;
And every turret, from your coming, rise
The mother of some great metropolis.

ALMANZOR
 'Tis pity, words, which none but gods should hear,
Should lose their sweetness in a soldier's ear:

I am not that Almanzor whom you praise;
But your fair mouth can fair ideas raise:—
I am a wretch, to whom it is denied
To accept, with honour, what I wish with pride;
And, since I light not for myself, must bring
The fruits of all my conquests to the king.

LYNDARAXA

Say rather to the queen, to whose fair name
I know you vow the trophies of your fame.
I hope she is as kind as she is fair;
Kinder than inexperienced virgins are
To their first loves; (though she has loved before,
And that first innocence is now no more:)
But, in revenge, she gives you all her heart,
(For you are much too brave to take a part.)
Though, blinded by a crown, she did not see
Almanzor greater than a king could be,
I hope her love repairs her ill-made choice:
Almanzor cannot be deluded twice.

ALMANZOR

 No, not deluded; for none count their gains,
Who, like Almanzor, frankly give their pains.

LYNDARAXA

Almanzor, do not cheat yourself, nor me;
Your love is not refined to that degree:
For, since you have desires, and those not blest,
Your love's uneasy, and at little rest.

ALMANZOR

 'Tis true, my own unhappiness I see;
But who, alas, can my physician be?
Love, like a lazy ague, I endure,
Which fears the water, and abhors the cure.

LYNDARAXA

'Tis a consumption, which your life does waste,
Still flattering you with hope, till help be past;
But, since of cure from her you now despair,
You, like consumptive men, should change your air:
Love somewhere else; 'tis a hard remedy,
But yet you owe yourself so much, to try.

ALMANZOR

 My love's now grown so much a part of me,
That life would, in the cure, endangered be:

At least, it like a limb cut off would show;
And better die than like a cripple go.

LYNDARAXA
You must be brought like madmen to their cure,
And darkness first, and next new bonds endure:
Do you dark absence to yourself ordain,
And I, in charity, will find the chain.

ALMANZOR
 Love is that madness which all lovers have;
But yet 'tis sweet and pleasing so to rave:
'Tis an enchantment, where the reason's bound;
But Paradise is in the enchanted ground;
A palace, void of envy, cares and strife,
Where gentle hours delude so much of life.
To take those charms away, and set me free,
Is but to send me into misery;
And prudence, of whose cure so much you boast,
Restores those pains, which that sweet folly lost.

LYNDARAXA
I would not, like philosophers, remove,
But show you a more pleasing shape of love.
You a sad, sullen, froward love did see;
I'll show him kind, and full of gaiety.
In short, Almanzor, it shall be my care
To show you love; for you but saw despair.

ALMANZOR
 I, in the shape of love, despair did see;
You, in his shape, would show inconstancy.

LYNDARAXA
There's no such thing as constancy you call;
Faith ties not hearts; 'tis inclination all.
Some wit deformed, or beauty much decayed,
First constancy in love a virtue made.
From friendship they that land-mark did remove,
And falsely placed it on the bounds of love.
Let the effects of change be only tried;
Court me, in jest, and call me Almahide:
But this is only counsel I impart,
For I, perhaps, should not receive your heart.

ALMANZOR
 Fair though you are
As summer mornings, and your eyes more bright

Than stars that twinkle in a winter's night;
Though you have eloquence to warm and move
Cold age, and praying hermits, into love;
Though Almahide with scorn rewards my care,—
Yet, than to change, 'tis nobler to despair.
My love's my soul; and that from fate is free;
'Tis that unchanged and deathless part of me.

LYNDARAXA
The fate of constancy your love pursue!
Still to be faithful to what's false to you.

[Turns from him, and goes off angrily.

ALMANZOR
Ye gods, why are not hearts first paired above,
But some still interfere in others' love!
Ere each for each by certain marks are known,
You mould them up in haste, and drop them down;
And, while we seek what carelessly you sort,
You sit in state, and make our pains your sport.

[Exeunt on both sides.

ACT IV

SCENE I

Enter **ABENAMAR**, and **SOLDIER**.

ABENAMAR
Haste and conduct the prisoner to my sight.

[Exit **SOLDIER**, and immediately enters with **SELIN** bound.

ABENAMAR
Did you, according to my orders, write? [To **SELIN**
And have you summoned Ozmyn to appear?

SELIN
I am not yet so much a slave to fear,
Nor has your son deserved so ill of me,
That by his death or bonds I would be free.

ABENAMAR
Against thy life thou dost the sentence give;

Behold how short a time thou hast to live.

SELIN
Make haste, and draw the curtain while you may;
You but shut out the twilight of my day.
Beneath the burden of my age I bend:
You kindly ease me ere my journey's end.

[To them a **SOLDIER** with **OZMYN**; **OZMYN** kneels.

ABENAMAR [to **SELIN**]
It is enough, my promise makes you free;
Resign your bonds, and take your liberty.

OZMYN
Sir, you are just, and welcome are these bands;
'Tis all the inheritance a son demands.

SELIN
Your goodness, O my Ozmyn, is too great;
I am not weary of my fetters yet:
Already, when you move me to resign,
I feel them heavier on your feet than mine.

[Enter another **SOLDIER**.

SOLDIER
A youth attends you in the outer room,
Who seems in haste, and does from Ozmyn come.

ABENAMAR
Conduct him in.—

OZMYN
Sent from Benzayda, I fear, to me.

[To them **BENZAYDA**, in the habit of a man.

BENZAYDA
My Ozmyn here!

OZMYN
Benzayda! 'tis she!—
Go youth, I have no business for thee here;
Go to the Albayzyn, and attend me there.
I'll not be long away; I pray thee go,
By all our love and friendship—

BENZAYDA

Ozmyn, no:
I did not take on me this bold disguise,
For ends so low, to cheat your watchmen's eyes.
When I attempted this, it was to do
An action, to be envied even by you;
But you, alas, have been too diligent,
And what I purposed fatally prevent!
Those chains, which for my father I would bear,
I take with less content to find you here;
Except your father will that mercy show,
That I may wear them both for him and you.

ABENAMAR

I thank thee, fortune! thou hast, in one hour,
Put all I could have asked thee in my power.
My own lost wealth thou giv'st not only back,
But driv'st upon my coast my pirate's wreck.

SELIN

With Ozmyn's kindness I was grieved before,
But yours, Benzayda, has' undone me more.

ABENAMAR [to a **SOLDIER**.

Go fetch new fetters, and the daughter bind.

OZMYN

Be just at least, sir, though you are not kind:
Benzayda is not as a prisoner brought,
But comes to suffer for another's fault.

ABENAMAR

Then, Ozmyn, mark, that justice which I do,
I, as severely, will exact from you:
The father is not wholly dead in me;
Or you may yet revive it, if it be.
Like tapers new blown out, the fumes remain,
To catch the light, and bring it back again.
Benzayda gave you life, and set you free;
For that, I will restore her liberty.

OZMYN

Sir, on my knees I thank you.

ABENAMAR

Ozmyn, hold;
One part of what I purpose is untold:
Consider, then, it on your part remains,

When I have broke, not to resume your chains.
Like an indulgent father, I have paid
All debts, which you, my prodigal, have made.
Now you are clear, break off your fond design,
Renounce Benzayda, and be wholly mine.

OZMYN
Are these the terms? Is this the liberty?
Ah, sir, how can you so inhuman be?
My duty to my life I will prefer;
But life and duty must give place to her.

ABENAMAR
Consider what you say, for, with one breath,
You disobey my will, and give her death.

OZMYN
Ah, cruel father, what do you propose!
Must I then kill Benzayda, or must lose?
I can do neither; in this wretched state.
The least that I can suffer is your hate;
And yet that's worse than death: Even while I sue,
And choose your hatred, I could die for you.
Break quickly, heart, or let my blood be spilt
By my own hand, to save a father's guilt.

BENZAYDA
Hear me, my lord, and take this wretched life,
To free you from the fear of Ozmyn's wife.
I beg but what with ease may granted be,
To spare your son, and kill your enemy;
Or, if my death's a grace too great to give,
Let me, my lord, without my Ozmyn live.
Far from your sight and Ozmyn's let me go,
And take from him a care, from you a foe.

OZMYN
How, my Benzayda! can you thus resign
That love, which you have vowed so firmly mine?
Can you leave me for life and liberty?

BENZAYDA
What I have done will show that I dare die;
But I'll twice suffer death, and go away,
Rather than make you wretched by my stay:
By this my father's freedom will be won;
And to your father I restore a son.

SELIN

Cease, cease, my children, your unhappy strife,
Selin will not be ransomed by your life.
Barbarian, thy old foe defies thy rage; [To **ABENAMAR**.
Turn, from their youth, thy malice to my age.

BENZAYDA

Forbear, dear father! for your Ozmyn's sake,
Do not such words to Ozmyn's father speak.

OZMYN

Alas, 'tis counterfeited rage; he strives
But to divert the danger from our lives:
For I can witness, sir, and you might see,
How in your person he considered me.
He still declined the combat where you were;
And you well know it was not out of fear.

BENZAYDA

Alas, my lord, where can your vengeance fall?
Your justice will not let it reach us all.
Selin and Ozmyn both would sufferers be;
And punishment's a favour done to me.
If we are foes, since you have power to kill,
'Tis generous in you not to have the will;
But, are we foes? Look round, my lord, and see;
Point out that face which is your enemy.
Would you your hand in Selin's blood embrue?
Kill him unarmed, who, armed, shunned killing you?
Am I your foe? Since you detest my line,
That hated name of Zegry I resign:
For you, Benzayda will herself disclaim;
Call me your daughter, and forget my name.

SELIN

This virtue would even savages subdue;
And shall it want the power to vanquish you?

OZMYN

It has, it has; I read it in his eyes;
'Tis now not anger, 'tis but shame denies;
A shame of error, that great spirits find,
When keeps down virtue struggling in the mind.

ABENAMAR

Yes, I am vanquished! The fierce conflict's past,
And shame itself is now o'ercome at last.
'Twas long before my stubborn mind was won;

But, melting once, I on the sudden run;
Nor can I hold my headlong kindness more,
Than I could curb my cruel rage before.

[Runs to **BENZAYDA**, and embraces her.

Benzayda, 'twas your virtue vanquished me;
That could alone surmount my cruelty.

[Runs to **SELIN**, and unbinds him.

Forgive me, Selin, my neglect of you;
But men, just waking, scarce know what they do.

OZMYN
O father!

BENZAYDA
Father!

ABENAMAR
Dare I own that name!
Speak, speak it often, to remove my shame.

[They all embrace him.

O Selin, O my children, let me go!
I have more kindness than I yet can show.
For my recovery I must shun your sight;
Eyes used to darkness cannot bear the light.

[He runs in, they following him.

SCENE II.—The Albayzyn.

Enter **ALMANZOR, ABDELMELECH, SOLDIERS.**

ALMANZOR
'Tis war again, and I am glad 'tis so;
Success shall now by force and courage go.
Treaties are but the combat of the brain,
Where still the stronger lose, and weaker gain.

ABDELMELECH
On this assault, brave sir, which we prepare,
Depends the sum and fortune of the war.

Encamped without the fort the Spaniard lies,
And may, in spite of us, send in supplies.
Consider yet, ere we attack the place,
What 'tis to storm it in an army's face.

ALMANZOR
The minds of heroes their own measures are,
They stand exempted from the rules of war.
One loose, one sally of the hero's soul,
Does all the military art controul;
While timorous wit goes round, or fords the shore,
He shoots the gulph, and is already o'er;
And, when the enthusiastic fit is spent,
Looks back amazed at what he underwent.

[Exeunt.

[An alarum within.

[Re-enter **ALMANZOR** and **ABDELMELECH**, with their **SOLDIERS.**

ABDELMELECH
They fly, they fly; take breath and charge again.

ALMANZOR
Make good your entrance, and bring up more men.
I feared, brave friend, my aid had been too late.

ABDELMELECH
You drew us from the jaws of certain fate.
At my approach,
The gate was open, and the draw-bridge down;
But, when they saw I stood, and came not on,
They charged with fury on my little band,
Who, much o'erpowered, could scarce the shock withstand.

ALMANZOR
Ere night we shall the whole Albayzyn gain.
But see, the Spaniards march along the plain
To its relief; you, Abdelmelech, go,
And force the rest, while I repulse the foe.

[Exit **ALMANZOR.**

[Enter **ABDALLA**, and some few **SOLDIERS**, who seem fearful.

ABDALLA
Turn cowards, turn! there is no hope in flight;

You yet may live, if you but dare to fight.
Come, you brave few, who only fear to fly,
We're not enough to conquer, but to die.

ABDELMELECH
No, prince, that mean advantage I refuse;
'Tis in your power a nobler fate to choose.
Since we are rivals, honour does command
We should not die, but by each other's hand.
Retire; and, if it prove my destiny [To his **MEN**.
To fall, I charge you let the prince go free.

[The **SOLDIERS** depart on both sides.

ABDALLA
O, Abdelmelech, that I knew some way
This debt of honour, which I owe, to pay!
But fate has left this only means for me,
To die, and leave you Lyndaraxa free.

ABDELMELECH
He, who is vanquished and is slain, is blest;
The wretched conqueror can ne'er have rest;
But is reserved a harder fate to prove.
Bound in the fetters of dissembled love.

ABDALLA
Now thou art base, and I deserve her more;
Without complaint I will to death adore.
Dar'st thou see faults, and yet dost love pretend?
I will even Lyndaraxa's crimes defend.

ABDELMELECH
Maintain her cause, then, better than thy own,—
Than thy ill got, and worse defended throne.

[They fight, **ABDALLA** falls.

ABDELMELECH
Now ask your life.

ABDALLA
'Tis gone; that busy thing,
The soul, is packing up, and just on wing,
Like parting swallows, when they seek the spring:
Like them, at its appointed time, it goes,
And flies to countries more unknown than those.

[Enter **LYNDARAXA** hastily, sees them, and is going out again. **ABDELMELECH** stops her.

ABDELMELECH
No, you shall stay, and see a sacrifice,
Not offered by my sword, but by your eyes.
From those he first ambitious poison drew,
And swelled to empire from the love of you.
Accursed fair!
Thy comet-blaze portends a prince's fate;
And suffering subjects groan beneath thy weight.

ABDALLA
Cease, rival, cease!
I would have forced you, but it wonnot be;
I beg you now, upbraid her not for me.
You, fairest, to my memory be kind![To **LYNDARAXA**.
Lovers like me your sex will seldom find.
When I usurped a crown for love of you,
I then did more, than, dying, now I do.
I'm still the same as when my love begun;
And, could I now this fate foresee or shun,
Would yet do all I have already done.

[Dies.

[She puts her handkerchief to her eyes.

ABDELMELECH
Weep on, weep on, for it becomes you now;
These tears you to that love may well allow.
His unrepenting soul, if it could move
Upward in crimes, flew spotted with your love;
And brought contagion to the blessed above.

LYNDARAXA
He's gone, and peace go with a constant mind!
His love deserved I should have been more kind;
But then your love and greater worth I knew:
I was unjust to him, but just to you.

ABDELMELECH
I was his enemy, and rival too,
Yet I some tears to his misfortune owe:
You owe him more; weep then, and join with me:
So much is due even to humanity.

LYNDARAXA
Weep for this wretch, whose memory I hate!

Whose folly made us both unfortunate!
Weep for this fool, who did my laughter move!
This whining, tedious, heavy lump of love!

ABDELMELECH
Had fortune favoured him, and frowned on me,
I then had been that heavy fool, not he:
Just this had been my funeral elegy.
Thy arts and falsehood I before did know,
But this last baseness was concealed till now;
And 'twas no more than needful to be known;
I could be cured by such an act alone.
My love, half blasted, yet in time would shoot;
But this last tempest rends it to the root.

LYNDARAXA
These little piques, which now your anger move,
Will vanish, and are only signs of love.
You've been too fierce; and, at some other time,
I should not with such ease forgive your crime:
But, in a day of public joy like this,
I pardon, and forget whate'er's amiss.

ABDELMELECH
These arts have oft prevailed, but must no more:
The spell is ended, and the enchantment o'er.
You have at last destroyed, with much ado,
That love, which none could have destroyed, but you.
My love was blind to your deluding art;
But blind men feel, when stabbed so near the heart.

LYNDARAXA
I must confess there was some pity due;
But I concealed it out of love to you.

ABDELMELECH
No, Lyndaraxa; 'tis at last too late:
Our loves have mingled with too much of fate.
I would, but cannot now, myself deceive:
O that you still could cheat, and I believe!

LYNDARAXA
Do not so light a quarrel long pursue:
You grieve your rival was less loved than you.
'Tis hard, when men of kindness must complain!

ABDELMELECH
I'm now awake, and cannot dream again.

LYNDARAXA
Yet hear—

ABDELMELECH
No more; nothing my heart can bend:
That queen, you scorned, you shall this night attend.
Your life the king has pardoned for my sake;
But on your pride I some revenge must take.
See now the effects of what your arts designed!
Thank your inconstant and ambitious mind.
'Tis just that she, who to no love is true,
Should be forsaken, and contemned, like you.

LYNDARAXA
All arts of injured women I will try:
First I will be revenged; and then I'll die.
But like some falling tower,
Whose seeming firmness does the sight beguile,
So hold I up my nodding head a while,
Till they come under; and reserve my fall,
That with my ruins I may reach them all,

ABDELMELECH
Conduct her hence.

[Exit **LYNDARAXA**. guarded.

[Enter a **SOLDIER**.

SOLDIER
Almanzor is victorious without fight;
The foes retreated when he came in sight.
Under the walls, this night, his men are drawn,
And mean to seek the Spaniard with the dawn.

ABDELMELECH
The sun's declined:
Command the watch be set without delay,
And in the fort let bold Benducar stay.—

[Exit **SOLDIER**.

I'll haste to court, where solitude I'll fly,
And herd, like wounded deer, in company.
But oh, how hard a passion to remove,
When I must shun myself, to 'scape from love!

[Exit.

ZULEMA, HAMET.

HAMET
 I thought your passion for the queen was dead,
 Or that your love had, with your hopes, been fled.

ZULEMA
 'Twas like a fire within a furnace pent:
 I smothered it, and kept it long from vent;
 But, fed with looks, and blown with sighs so fast,
 It broke a passage through my lips at last.

HAMET
 Where found you confidence your suit to move?
 Our broken fortunes are not fit to love.
 Well; you declared your love·—What followed then?

ZULEMA
 She looked as judges do on guilty men,
 When big with fate they triumph in their dooms,
 And smile before the deadly sentence comes.
 Silent I stood, as I were thunder-struck;
 Condemned and executed with a look.

HAMET
 You must, with haste, some remedy prepare:
 Now you are in, you must break through the snare.

ZULEMA
 She said, she would my folly yet conceal;
 But vowed my next attempt she would reveal.

HAMET
 'Tis dark; and in this lonely gallery,
 Remote from noise, and shunning every eye,
 One hour each evening she in private mourns,
 And prays, and to the circle then returns.

ZULEMA
 These lighted tapers show the time is nigh.
 Perhaps my courtship will not be in vain:
 At least, few women will of force complain.

[At the other end of the Gallery, enter **ALMANZOR** and **ESPERANZA**.

HAMET
Almanzor, and with him
The favourite slave of the sultana queen.

ZULEMA
Ere they approach, let us retire unseen,
And watch our time when they return again:
Then force shall give, if favour does deny;
And, that once done, we'll to the Spaniards fly.

[Exeunt **ZULEMA** and **HAMET**.

ALMANZOR
Now stand; the apartment of the queen is near;
And, from this place, your voice will reach her ear.

[**ESPERANZA** goes out.

SONG, IN TWO PARTS.

I.
He. How unhappy a lover am I,
While I sigh for my Phillis in vain;
All my hopes of delight
Are another man's right,
Who is happy, while I am in pain!

II.
She. Since her honour allows no relief,
But to pity the pains which you bear,
'Tis the best of your fate
In a hopeless estate,
To give o'er, and betimes to despair.

III.
He. I have tried the false med'cine in vain;
For I wish what I hope not to win:
From without, my desire
Has no food to its fire;
But it burns and consumes me within.

IV.
She. Yet, at least, 'tis a pleasure to know
That you are not unhappy alone:
For the nymph you adore

Is as wretched, and more;
And counts all your sufferings her own.

V.
He. O ye gods, let me suffer for both;
At the feet of my Phyllis I'll lie:
I'll resign up my breath,
And take pleasure in death
To be pitied by her when I die.

VI.
She. What her honour denied you in life,
In her death she will give to your love.
Such flame as is true
After fate will renew,
For the souls to meet closer above.

[Enter **ESPERANZA** again, after the Song.

ALMANZOR
Accept this diamond, till I can present
Something more worthy my acknowledgement.
And now farewell: I will attend, alone,
Her coming forth; and make my sufferings known.

[Exit **ESPERANZA**.

A hollow wind comes whistling through that door,
And a cold shivering seizes me all o'er;
My teeth, too, chatter with a sudden fright:—
These are the raptures of too fierce delight,
The combat of the tyrants, hope and fear;
Which hearts, for want of field-room, cannot bear.
I grow impatient;—this, or that's the room:—
I'll meet her;—now methinks, I her her come.

[He goes to the door; the **GHOST OF HIS MOTHER** meets him: He starts back: The **GHOST** stands in the door.

Well may'st thou make thy boast, whate'er thou art!
Thou art the first e'er made Almanzor start.
My legs
Shall bear me to thee in their own despite:
I'll rush into the covert of thy night,
And pull thee backward, by the shroud, to light;
Or else I'll squeeze thee, like a bladder, there,
And make thee groan thyself away to air.

[The **GHOST** retires.

So, thou art gone! Thou canst no conquest boast:
I thought what was the courage of a ghost.—
The grudging of my ague yet remains;
My blood, like icicles, hangs in my veins,
And does not drop:—Be master of that door,
We two will not disturb each other more.
I erred a little, but extremes may join;
That door was hell's, but this is heaven's and mine.

[Goes to the other door, and is met again by the **GHOST**.

Again! by heaven, I do conjure thee, speak!
What art thou, spirit? and what dost thou seek?

[The **GHOST** comes on softly after the conjuration; and **ALMANZOR** retires to the middle of the stage.

GHOST
I am the ghost of her who gave thee birth;
The airy shadow of her mouldering earth.
Love of thy father me through seas did guide;
On seas I bore thee, and on seas I died.
I died; and for my winding sheet a wave
I had, and all the ocean for my grave.
But, when my soul to bliss did upward move,
I wandered round the crystal walls above;
But found the eternal fence so steeply high,
That, when I mounted to the middle sky,
I flagged, and fluttered down, and could not fly.
Then, from the battlements of the heavenly tower,
A watchman angel bid me wait this hour;
And told me, I had yet a task assigned,
To warn that little pledge I left behind;
And to divert him, ere it were too late,
From crimes unknown, and errors of his fate.

ALMANZOR
 Speak, holy shade; thou parent-form, speak on!

[Bowing.

Instruct thy mortal-elemented son;
For here I wander, to myself unknown.
But O, thou better part of heavenly air,
Teach me, kind spirit, since I'm still thy care,
My parents' names:
If I have yet a father, let me know

To whose old age my humble youth must bow,
And pay its duty, if he mortal be,
Or adoration, if a mind, like thee.

GHOST
Then, what I may, I'll tell.—
From ancient blood thy father's lineage springs,
Thy mother's thou deriv'st from stems of kings.
A Christian born, and born again that day,
When sacred water washed thy sins away.
Yet, bred in errors, thou dost misemploy
That strength heaven gave thee, and its flock destroy.

ALMANZOR
 By reason, man a godhead may discern,
But how he should be worshipped cannot learn.

GHOST
Heaven does not now thy ignorance reprove,
But warns thee from known crimes of lawless love.
That crime thou knowest, and, knowing, dost not shun,
Shall an unknown and greater crime pull on:
But if, thus warned, thou leav'st this cursed place,
Then shalt thou know the author of thy race.
Once more I'll see thee; then my charge is done.
Far hence, upon the mountains of the moon,
Is my abode; where heaven and nature smile,
And strew with flowers the secret bed of Nile.
Blessed souls are there refined, and made more bright,
And, in the shades of heaven, prepared for light.

[Exit **GHOST**.

ALMANZOR
 O heaven, how dark a riddle's thy decree,
Which bounds our wills, yet seems to leave them free!
Since thy fore-knowledge cannot be in vain,
Our choice must be what thou didst first ordain.
Thus, like a captive in an isle confined,
Man walks at large, a prisoner of the mind:
Wills all his crimes, while heaven the indictment draws,
And, pleading guilty, justifies the laws.
Let fate be fate; the lover and the brave
Are ranked, at least, above the vulgar slave.
Love makes me willing to my death to run;
And courage scorns the death it cannot shun.

[Enter **ALMAHIDE** with a taper.

ALMAHIDE

My light will sure discover those who talk.—
Who dares to interrupt my private walk?

ALMANZOR

 He, who dares love, and for that love must die,
And, knowing this, dares yet love on, am I.

ALMAHIDE

That love which you can hope, and I can pay,
May be received and given in open day:
My praise and my esteem you had before;
And you have bound yourself to ask no more.

ALMANZOR

 Yes, I have bound myself; but will you take
The forfeit of that bond, which force did make?

ALMAHIDE

You know you are from recompence debarred;
But purest love can live without reward.

ALMANZOR

 Pure love had need be to itself a feast;
For, like pure elements, 'twill nourish least.

ALMAHIDE

It therefore yields the only pure content;
For it, like angels, needs no nourishment.
To eat and drink can no perfection be;
All appetite implies necessity.

ALMANZOR

 'Twere well, if I could like a spirit live;
But, do not angels food to mortals give?
What if some demon should my death foreshow,
Or bid me change, and to the Christians go;
Will you not think I merit some reward,
When I my love above my life regard?

ALMAHIDE

In such a case your change must be allowed:
I would myself dispense with what you vowed.

ALMANZOR

 Were I to die that hour when I possess,
This minute shall begin my happiness.

ALMAHIDE

The thoughts of death your passion would remove;
Death is a cold encouragement to love.

ALMANZOR

No; from my joys I to my death would run,
And think the business of my life well done:
But I should walk a discontented ghost,
If flesh and blood were to no purpose lost.

ALMAHIDE

You love me not, Almanzor; if you did,
You would not ask what honour must forbid.

ALMANZOR

And what is honour, but a love well hid?

ALMAHIDE

Yes, 'tis the conscience of an act well done,
Which gives us power our own desires to shun;
The strong and secret curb of headlong will;
The self-reward of good, and shame of ill.

ALMANZOR

These, madam, are the maxims of the day,
When honour's present, and when love's away.
The duty of poor honour were too hard,
In arms all day, at night to mount the guard.
Let him, in pity, now to rest retire;
Let these soft hours be watched by warm desire.

ALMAHIDE

Guards, who all day on painful duty keep,
In dangers are not privileged to sleep.

ALMANZOR

And with what dangers are you threatened here?
Am I, alas! a foe for you to fear?
See, madam, at your feet this enemy;

[Kneels.

Without your pity and your love I die.

ALMAHIDE

Rise, rise, and do not empty hopes pursue;
Yet think that I deny myself, not you.

ALMANZOR

A happiness so high I cannot bear:
My love's too fierce, and you too killing fair.
I grow enraged to see such excellence!—
If words, so much disordered, give offence,
My love's too full of zeal to think of sense.
Be you like me; dull reason hence remove,
And tedious forms, and give a loose to love.
Love eagerly; let us be gods to-night;
And do not, with half yielding, clash delight.

ALMAHIDE

Thou strong seducer, opportunity!
Of womankind, half are undone by thee!
Though I resolve I will not be misled,
I wish I had not heard what you have said!
I cannot be so wicked to comply;
And, yet, am most unhappy to deny!
Away!

ALMANZOR

I will not move me from this place:
I can take no denial from that face!

ALMAHIDE

If I could yield,—but think not that I will,—
You and myself I in revenge should kill;
For I should hate us both, when it were done,
And would not to the shame of life be won.

ALMANZOR

Live but to-night, and trust to-morrow's mind:
Ere that can come, there's a whole life behind.
Methinks, already crowned with joys I lie,
Speechless and breathless, in an ecstasy!
Not absent in one thought: I am all there:
Still close, yet wishing still to be more near.

ALMAHIDE

Deny your own desires; for it will be
Too little now to be denied by me.
Will he, who does all great, all noble seem,
Be lost and forfeit to his own esteem?
Will he, who may with heroes claim a place,
Belie that fame, and to himself be base?
Think how august and godlike you did look,
When my defence, unbribed, you undertook;

But, when an act so brave you disavow,
How little, and how mercenary now!

ALMANZOR
Are, then, my services no higher prized?
And can I fall so low, to be despised?

ALMAHIDE
Yes; for whatever may be bought, is low;
And you yourself, who sell yourself, are so.
Remember the great act you did this day:
How did your love to virtue then give way!
When you gave freedom to my captive lord,—
That rival who possessed what you adored,—
Of such a deed what price can there be made?
Think well; is that an action to be paid?
It was a miracle of virtue shown;
And wonders are with wonder paid alone.
And would you all that secret joy of mind,
Which great souls only in great actions find,
All that, for one tumultuous minute lose?

ALMANZOR
I would that minute before ages chuse.
Praise is the pay of heaven for doing good;
But love's the best return for flesh and blood.

ALMAHIDE
You've moved my heart so much, I can deny
No move; but know, Almanzor, I can die.
Thus far my virtue yields; if I have shown
More love than what I ought, let this atone.

[Going to stab herself.

ALMANZOR
Hold, hold!
Such fatal proofs of love you shall not give:
Deny me; hate me; both are just,—but live!
Your virtue I will ne'er disturb again;
Nor dare to ask, for fear I should obtain.

ALMAHIDE
'Tis generous to have conquered your desire;
You mount above your wish, and lose it higher.
There's pride in virtue, and a kindly heat;
Not feverish, like your love, but full as great.
Farewell; and may our loves hereafter be

But image-like, to heighten piety.

ALMANZOR
'Tis time I should be gone.—
Alas! I am but half converted yet;
All I resolve, I with one look forget;
And, like a lion, whom no arts can tame,
Shall tear even those, who would my rage reclaim.

[Exeunt severally.

[**ZULEMA** and **HAMET** watch **ALMANZOR**; and when he is gone, go in after the **QUEEN**.

[Enter **ABDELMELECH** and **LYNDARAXA**.

LYNDARAXA
It is enough, you've brought me to this place:
Here stop, and urge no further my disgrace.
Kill me; in death your mercy will be seen,
But make me not a captive to the queen.

ABDELMELECH
'Tis therefore I this punishment provide:
This only can revenge me on your pride.
Prepare to suffer what you shun in vain;
And know, you now are to obey, not reign.

[Enter **ALMAHIDE** shrieking; her hair loose; she runs over the stage.

ALMAHIDE
Help, help, O heaven, some help!

[Enter **ZULEMA** and **HAMET**.

ZULEMA
Make haste before,
And intercept her passage to the door.

ABDELMELECH
Villains, what act are you attempting here!

ALMANZOR
I thank thee, heaven! some succour does appear.

[As **ABDELMELECH** is going to help the **QUEEN**, **LYNDARAXA** pulls out his sword, and holds it.

ABDELMELECH
With what ill fate my good design is curst!

ZULEMA
We have no time to think; dispatch him first.

ABDELMELECH
O for a sword!

[They make at **ABDELMELECH**; he goes off at one door, while the **QUEEN** escapes at the other.

ZULEMA
Ruined!

HAMET
 Undone!

LYNDARAXA
And, which is worst of all,
He is escaped.

ZULEMA
I hear them loudly call.

LYNDARAXA
Your fear will lose you; call as loud as they:
I have not time to teach you what to say.
The court will in a moment all be here;
But second what I say, and do not fear.
Call help; run that way; leave the rest to me.

[**ZULEMA** and **HAMET** retire, and within cry,—Help!

[Enter, at several doors, the **KING**, **ABENAMAR**, **SELIN**, **OZMYN**, **ALMANZOR**, with **GUARDS** attending **BOABDELIN**.

BOABDELIN
What can the cause of all this tumult be?
And what the meaning of that naked sword?

LYNDARAXA
I'll tell, when fear will so much breath afford.—
The queen and Abdelmelech—'Twill not out—
Even I, who saw it, of the truth yet doubt,
It seems so strange.

ALMANZOR
 Did she not name the queen?
Haste; speak.

LYNDARAXA

How dare I speak what I have seen?—
With Hamet, and with Zulema I went,
To pay both theirs, and my acknowledgment
To Almahide, and by her mouth implore
Your clemency, our fortunes to restore.
We chose this hour, which we believed most free,
When she retired from noise and company.
The ante-chamber past, we gently knocked,
Unheard it seems, but found the lodgings locked,
In duteous silence while we waited there,
We first a noise, and then long whispers hear;
Yet thought it was the queen at prayers alone,
Till she distinctly said,—If this were known,
My love, what shame, what danger would ensue!
Yet I,—and sighed,—could venture more for you!

BOABDELIN

O heaven, what do I hear!

ALMANZOR

 Let her go on.

LYNDARAXA

And how,—then murmured in a bigger tone
Another voice,—and how should it be known?
This hour is from your court attendants free;
The king suspects Almanzor, but not me.

ZULEMA

I find her drift; Hamet, be confident;

[At the door.

Second her words, and fear not the event.

ZULEMA and **HAMET** enter. The **KING** embraces them.

BOABDELIN

Welcome, my only friends;—behold in me,
O kings, behold the effects of clemency!
See here the gratitude of pardoned foes!
That life, I gave them, they for me expose!

HAMET

 Though Abdelmelech was our friend before,
When duty called us, he was so no more.

ALMANZOR

Damn your delay!—you torturers, proceed!
I will not hear one word but Almahide.

BOABDELIN

When you, within, the traitor's voice did hear,
What did you then?

ZULEMA

I durst not trust my ear;
But, peeping through the key-hole, I espied
The queen, and Abdelmelech by her side;
She on the couch, he on her bosom lay;
Her hand about his neck his head did stay,
And from his forehead wiped the drops away.

BOABDELIN

Go on, go on, my friends, to clear my doubt;
I hope I shall have life to hear you out.

ZULEMA

What had been, sir, you may suspect too well;
What followed, modesty forbids to tell:
Seeing what we had thought beyond belief,
Our hearts so swelled with anger and with grief,
That, by plain force, we strove the door to break.
He, fearful, and with guilt, or love, grown weak,
Just as we entered, 'scaped the other way;
Nor did the amazed queen behind him stay.

LYNDARAXA

His sword, in so much haste, he could not mind;
But left this witness of his crime behind.

BOABDELIN

O proud, ungrateful, faithless womankind!
How changed, and what a monster am I made!
My love, my honour, ruined and betrayed!

ALMANZOR

Your love and honour! mine are ruined worse:—
Furies and hell!—What right have you to curse?
Dull husband as you are,
What can your love, or what your honour, be?
I am her lover, and she's false to me.

BOABDELIN

Go; when the authors of my shame are found,

Let them be taken instantly and bound:
They shall be punished as our laws require:
'Tis just, that flames should be condemned to fire.
This, with the dawn of morning shall be done.

ABENAMAR

You haste too much her execution.
Her condemnation ought to be deferred;
With justice, none can be condemned unheard.

BOABDELIN

A formal process tedious is, and long;
Besides, the evidence is full and strong.

LYNDARAXA

The law demands two witnesses; and she
Is cast, for which heaven knows I grieve, by three.

OZMYN

Hold, sir! since you so far insist on law,
We can from thence one just advantage draw:
That law, which dooms adultresses to die,
Gives champions, too, to slandered chastity.

ALMANZOR

And how dare you, who from my bounty live,
Intrench upon my love's prerogative?
Your courage in your own concernments try;
Brothers are things remote, while I am by.

OZMYN

I knew not you thus far her cause would own,
And must not suffer you to fight alone:
Let two to two in equal combat join;
You vindicate her person, I her line.

LYNDARAXA

Of all mankind, Almanzor has least right
In her defence, who wrong'd his love, to fight.

ALMANZOR

'Tis false: she is not ill, nor can she be;
She must be chaste, because she's loved by me.

ZULEMA

Dare you, what sense and reason prove, deny?

ALMANZOR

When she's in question, sense and reason lie.

ZULEMA
For truth, and for my injured sovereign,
What I have said, I will to death maintain.

OZMYN
So foul a falsehood, whoe'er justifies,
Is basely born, and, like a villain, lies.
In witness of that truth, be this my gage.

[Takes a ring from his finger.

HAMET
 I take it; and despise a traitor's rage.

BOABDELIN
The combat's yours.—A guard the lists surround;
Then raise a scaffold in the encompassed ground,
And, by it, piles of wood; in whose just fire,
Her champions slain, the adultress shall expire.

ABENAMAR
We ask no favour, but what arms will yield.

BOABDELIN
Choose, then, two equal judges of the field:
Next morning shall decide the doubtful strife,
Condemn the unchaste, or quit the virtuous wife.

ALMANZOR
 But I am both ways cursed:
For Almahide must die, if I am slain;
Or for my rival I the conquest gain.

[Exeunt.

ACT V

SCENE I

ALMANZOR solus.

I have outfac'd myself; and justified,
What I knew false, to all the world beside.
She was as faithless as her sex could be;

And, now I am alone, she's so to me.
She's fallen! and, now, where shall we virtue find?
She was the last that stood of womankind.
Could she so holily my flames remove,
And fall that hour to Abdelmelech's love?
Yet her protection I must undertake;
Not now for love, but for my honour's sake,
That moved me first, and must oblige me still:
My cause is good, however her's be ill.
I'll leave her, when she's freed; and let it be
Her punishment, she could be false to me.

[To him **ABDELMELECH**, guarded.

ABDELMELECH
Heaven is not heaven, nor are there deities
There is some new rebellion in the skies.
All that was good and holy is dethroned,
And lust and rapine are for justice owned.

ALMANZOR
 'Tis true; what justice in that heaven can be,
Which thus affronts me with the sight of thee?
Why must I be from just revenge debarred?
Chains are thy arms, and prisons are thy guard:
The death, thou diest, may to a husband be
A satisfaction; but 'tis none to me.
My love would justice to itself afford;
But now thou creep'st to death below my sword.

ABDELMELECH
This threatening would show better were I free.

ALMANZOR
 No; wert thou freed, I would not threaten thee;
This arm should then—but now it is too late!
I could redeem thee to a nobler fate.
As some huge rock,
Rent from its quarry, does the waves divide,
So I
Would souse upon thy guards, and dash them wide:
Then, to my rage left naked and alone,
Thy too much freedom thou should'st soon bemoan:
Dared like a lark, that, on the open plain
Pursued and cuffed, seeks shelter now in vain;
So on the ground wouldst thou expecting lie,
Not daring to afford me victory.
But yet thy fate's not ripe; it is decreed,

Before thou diest, that Almahide be freed.
My honour first her danger must remove,
And then revenge on thee my injured love.

[Exeunt severally.

SCENE II

The SCENE changes to the Vivarambla, and appears filled with **SPECTATORS**; a Scaffold hung with black.

Enter the **QUEEN** guarded, with **ESPERANZA**.

ALMAHIDE
See how the gazing people crowd the place,
All gaping to be filled with my disgrace.

[A shout within.

That shout, like the hoarse peals of vultures, rings,
When over fighting fields they beat their wings.—
Let never woman trust in innocence,
Or think her chastity its own defence;
Mine has betrayed me to this public shame,
And virtue, which I served, is but a name.

ESPERANZA
 Leave then that shadow, and for succour fly
To Him we serve, the Christian's Deity.
Virtue's no god, nor has she power divine:
But He protects it, who did first enjoin.
Trust then in Him; and from his grace implore
Faith to believe, what rightly we adore.

ALMAHIDE
Thou Power unknown, if I have erred, forgive!
My infancy was taught what I believe.
But if the Christians truly worship thee,
Let me thy Godhead in thy succour see:
So shall thy justice in my safety shine,
And all my days, which thou shalt add, be thine!

[Enter the **KING**, **ABENAMAR**, **LYNDARAXA**, **BENZAYDA**: then **ABDELMELECH** guarded; and after him
SELIN and **ALABEZ**, as Judges of the Field.

BOABDELIN
You, judges of the field, first take your place.—

The accusers and accused bring face to face.
Set guards, and let the lists be opened wide;
And may just heaven assist the juster side!

ALMAHIDE
What! not one tender look, one passing word?
Farewell, my much unkind, but still loved lord!
Your throne was for my humble fate too high,
And therefore heaven thinks fit that I should die.
My story be forgot, when I am dead,
Lest it should fright some other from your bed;
And, to forget me, may you soon adore
Some happier maid,—yet none could love you more.
But may you never think me innocent,
Lest it should cause you trouble to repent.

BOABDELIN
'Tis pity so much beauty should not live; [Aside.
Yet I too much am injured, to forgive.

[Goes to his seat.

[Trumpets: Then enter two **MOORS**, bearing two naked swords before the accusers **ZULEMA** and **HAMET**, who follow them. The **JUDGES** seat themselves; the **QUEEN** and **ABDELMELECH** are led to the Scaffold.

ALABEZ
 Say for what end you thus in arms appear;
What are your names, and what demand you here?

ZULEMA
The Zegrys' ancient race our lineage claims;
And Zulema and Hamet are our names.
Like loyal subjects in these lists we stand,
And justice in our king's behalf demand.

HAMET
 For whom, in witness of what both have seen,
Bound by our duty, we appeach the queen
And Abdelmelech, of adultery.

ZULEMA
Which, like true knights, we will maintain, or die.

ALABEZ
 Swear on the Alcoran your cause is right,
And Mahomet so prosper you in fight.

[They touch their foreheads with the Alcoran, and bow.

[Trumpets on the other side of the Stage; two **MOORS**, as before, with bare swords before **ALMANZOR** and **OZMYN**.

SELIN
Say for what end you thus in arms appear;
What are your names, and what demand you here?

ALMANZOR
Ozmyn is his, Almanzor is my name;
We come as champions of the queen's fair fame.

OZMYN
To prove these Zegrys, like false traitors, lie;
Which, like true knights, we will maintain, or die.

SELIN [to **ALMAHIDE**.]
Madam, do you for champions take these two,
By their success to live or die?

ALMANZOR
I do.

SELIN
Swear on the Alcoran your cause is right;
And Mahomet so prosper you in fight.

[They kiss the Alcoran.

[**OZMYN** and **BENZAYDA** embrace, and take leave in dumb show; while **LYNDARAXA** speaks to her Brother.

LYNDARAXA
If you o'ercome, let neither of them live,
But use with care the advantages I give:
One of their swords in fight shall useless be;
The bearer of it is suborned by me.

[She and **BENZAYDA** retire.

ALABEZ
Now, principals and seconds, all advance,
And each of you assist his fellow's chance.

SELIN
The wind and sun we equally divide,
So let the event of arms the truth decide.

The chances of the fight, and every wound,
The trumpets, on the victor's part, resound.

[The Trumpets sound; **ALMANZOR** and **ZULEMA** meet and fight; **OZMYN** and **HAMET**. After some passes, the sword of **OZMYN** breaks; he retires, defending himself, and is wounded; the Zegrys'

[Trumpets sound their advantage. **ALMANZOR**, in the mean time, drives **ZULEMA** to the farther end of the Stage, till, hearing the Trumpets of the adverse Party, he looks back, and sees **OZMYN'S** misfortune; he makes at **ZULEMA** just as **OZMYN** falls, in retiring, and **HAMET** is thrusting at him.

HAMET [To **OZMYN**, thrusting.]
Our difference now shall soon determined be.

ALMANZOR
Hold, traitor, and defend thyself from me.

[**HAMET** leaves **OZMYN** (who cannot rise), and both he and **ZULEMA** fall on **ALMANZOR**, and press him; he retires, and **HAMET**, advancing first, is run through the body, and falls. The Queen's Trumpets sound. **ALMANZOR** pursues **ZULEMA**.

LYNDARAXA
I must make haste some remedy to find:—
Treason, Almanzor, treason! look behind.

[**ALMANZOR** looks behind him to see who calls, and **ZULEMA** takes the advantage, and wounds him; the Zegrys' Trumpets sound; **ALMANZOR** turns upon **ZULEMA**, and wounds him; he falls. The Queens Trumpets sound.

ALMANZOR
Now triumph in thy sister's treachery.

[Stabbing him.

ZULEMA
Hold, hold! I have enough to make me die,
But, that I may in peace resign my breath,
I must confess my crime before my death.
Mine is the guilt; the queen is innocent:
I loved her, and, to compass my intent,
Used force, which Abdelmelech did prevent.
The lie my sister forged; but, O! my fate
Comes on too soon, and I repent too late.
Fair queen, forgive; and let my penitence
Expiate some part of—

[Dies.

ALMANZOR

Even thy whole offence!
[To the **JUDGES**.]
If aught remains in the sultana's cause,
I here am ready to fulfil the laws.

SELIN
The law is fully satisfied, and we
Pronounce the queen and Abdelmelech free.

ABDELMELECH
Heaven, thou art just!

[The **JUDGES** rise from their seats, and go before **ALMANZOR** to the Queens Scaffold; he unbinds the **QUEEN** and **ABDELMELECH**; they all go off, the **PEOPLE** shouting, and the Trumpets sounding the while.

BOABDELIN
Before we pay our thanks, or show our joy,
Let us our needful charity employ.
Some skilful surgeon speedily be found,
To apply fit remedies to Ozmyn's wound.

BENZAYDA [running to **OZMYN**.]
That be my charge: my linen I will tear;
Wash it with tears, and bind it with my hair.

OZMYN
With how much pleasure I my pains endure,
And bless the wound which causes such a cure!

[Exit **OZMYN** led by **BENZAYDA** and **ABDELMELECH**.

BOABDELIN
Some from the place of combat bear the slain.—
Next Lyndaraxa's death I should ordain:
But let her, who this mischief did contrive,
For ever banished from Granada live.

LYNDARAXA
Thou shouldst have punished more, or not at all:
By her thou hast not ruined, thou shalt fall.
The Zegrys shall revenge their branded line,
Betray their gate, and with the Christians join. [Aside.

[Exit **LYNDARAXA** with **ALABEZ**; the bodies of her **BROTHERS** are borne after her.

[**ALMANZOR**, **ALMAHIDE**, and **ESPERANZA**, re-enter to the **KING**.

ALMAHIDE
The thanks thus paid, which first to heaven were due,
My next, Almanzor, let me pay to you:
Somewhat there is of more concernment too,
Which 'tis not fit you should in public know.
First let your wounds be dressed with speedy care,
And then you shall the important secret share.

ALMANZOR
 Whene'er you speak,
Were my wounds mortal, they should still bleed on;
And I would listen till my life were gone:
My soul should even for your last accent stay,
And then shout out, and with such speed obey,
It should not bait at heaven to stop its way.

[Exit **ALMANZOR**.

BOABDELIN
'Tis true, Almanzor did her honour save,
But yet what private business can they have?
Such freedom virtue will not sure allow;
I cannot clear my heart, but must my brow. [Aside.

[He approaches **ALMAHIDE**.

Welcome again, my virtuous, loyal wife;
Welcome to love, to honour, and to life!

[Goes to salute her, she starts back.

You seem
As if you from a loathed embrace did go!

ALMAHIDE
Then briefly will I speak, since you must know
What to the world my future acts will show:
But hear me first, and then my reasons weigh.
'Tis known, how duty led me to obey
My father's choice; and how I since did live,
You, sir, can best your testimony give.
How to your aid I have Almanzor brought,
When by rebellious crowds your life was sought;
Then, how I bore your causeless jealousy,
(For I must speak) and after set you free,
When you were prisoner in the chance of war:
These, sure, are proofs of love.

BOABDELIN

I grant they are.

ALMAHIDE

And could you then, O cruelly unkind!
So ill reward such tenderness of mind?
Could you, denying what our laws afford
The meanest subject, on a traitor's word,
Unheard, condemn, and suffer me to go
To death, and yet no common pity show!

BOABDELIN

Love filled my heart even to the brim before;
And then, with too much jealousy, boiled o'er.

ALMAHIDE

Be't love or jealousy, 'tis such a crime,
That I'm forewarned to trust a second time.
Know, then, my prayers to heaven shall never cease,
To crown your arms in war, your wars with peace;
But from this day I will not know your bed:
Though Almahide still lives, your wife is dead;
And with her dies a love so pure and true,
It could be killed by nothing but by you.

[Exit **ALMAHIDE**.

BOABDELIN

Yes; you will spend your life in prayers for me,
And yet this hour my hated rival see.
She might a husband's jealousy forgive;
But she will only for Almanzor live.
It is resolved; I will myself provide
That vengeance, which my useless laws denied;
And, by Almanzor's death, at once remove
The rival of my empire, and my love.

[Exit **BOABDELIN.**

[Enter **ALMAHIDE**, led by **ALMANZOR**, and followed by **ESPERANZA**; she speaks, entering.

ALMAHIDE

How much, Almanzor, to your aid I owe,
Unable to repay, I blush to know;
Yet, forced by need, ere I can clear that score,
I, like ill debtors, come to borrow more.

ALMANZOR

Your new commands I on my knees attend:
I was created for no other end.
Born to be yours, I do by nature serve,
And, like the labouring beast, no thanks deserve.

ALMAHIDE

Yet first your virtue to your succour call,
For in this hard command you'll need it all.

ALMANZOR

I stand prepared; and whatsoe'er it be,
Nothing is hard to him, who loves like me.

ALMAHIDE

Then know, I from your love must yet implore
One proof:—that you would never see me more.

ALMANZOR

I must confess,

[Starting back.

For this last stroke I did no guard provide;
I could suspect no foe was near that side.
From winds and thickening clouds we thunder fear,
None dread it from that quarter which is clear;
And I would fain believe, 'tis but your art
To shew
You knew where deepest you could wound my heart.

ALMAHIDE

So much respect is to your passion due,
That sure I could not practise arts on you.
But that you may not doubt what I have said,
This hour I have renounced my husband's bed:
Judge, then, how much my fame would injured be,
If, leaving him, I should a lover see.

ALMANZOR

If his unkindness have deserved that curse,
Must I, for loving well, be punished worse?

ALMAHIDE

Neither your love nor merits I compare,
But my unspotted name must be my care.

ALMANZOR

I have this day established its renown.

ALMAHIDE

Would you so soon, what you have raised, throw down?

ALMANZOR

But, madam, is not yours a greater guilt,
To ruin him, who has that fabric built?

ALMAHIDE

No lover should his mistress' prayers withstand,
Yet you contemn my absolute command.

ALMANZOR

'Tis not contempt,
When your command is issued out too late;
'Tis past my power, and all beyond is fate.
I scarce could leave you, when to exile sent,
Much less when now recalled from banishment;
For if that heat your glances cast were strong,
Your eyes, like glasses, fire, when held so long.

ALMAHIDE

Then, since you needs will all my weakness know,
I love you; and so well, that you must go.
I am so much obliged, and have withal
A heart so boundless and so prodigal,
I dare not trust myself, or you, to stay,
But, like frank gamesters, must forswear the play.

ALMANZOR

Fate, thou art kind to strike so hard a blow:
I am quite stunned, and past all feeling now.
Yet—can you tell me you have power and will
To save my life, and at that instant kill?

ALMAHIDE

This, had you staid, you never must have known;
But, now you go, I may with honour own.

ALMANZOR

But, madam, I am forced to disobey:
In your defence my honour bids me stay.
I promised to secure your life and throne,
And, heaven be thanked, that work is yet undone.

ALMAHIDE

I here make void that promise which you made,
For now I have no farther need of aid.

That vow, which to my plighted lord was given,
I must not break, but may transfer to heaven:
I will with vestals live:
There needs no guard at a religious door;
Few will disturb the praying and the poor.

ALMANZOR
 Let me but near that happy temple stay,
And through the grates peep on you once a day;
To famished hope I would no banquet give:
I cannot starve, and wish but just to live.
Thus, as a drowning man
Sinks often, and does still more faintly rise,
With his last hold catching whate'er he spies;
So, fallen from those proud hopes I had before,
Your aid I for a dying wretch implore.

ALMAHIDE
I cannot your hard destiny withstand,

[**BOABDELIN**, and **GUARDS** above.

But slip, like bending rushes, from your hand.
Sink all at once, since you must sink at last.

ALMANZOR
 Can you that last relief of sight remove,
And thrust me out the utmost line of love!
Then, since my hopes of happiness are gone,
Denied all favours, I will seize this one.

[Catches her hand, and kisses it.

BOABDELIN
My just revenge no longer I'll forbear:
I've seen too much; I need not stay to hear.

[Descends.

ALMANZOR
 As a small shower
To the parched earth does some refreshment give,
So, in the strength of this, one day I'll live:
A day,—a year,—an age,—for ever, now;

[Betwixt each word he kisses her hand by force; she struggling.

I feel from every touch a new soul flow.

[She snatches her hand away.

My hoped eternity of joy is past!
'Twas insupportable, and could not last.
Were heaven not made of less, or duller joy,
'Twould break each minute, and itself destroy.

[Enter **KING** and **GUARDS**, below.

BOABDELIN
This, this, is he, for whom thou didst deny
To share my bed:—Let them together die.

ALMANZOR
Hear me, my lord.

BOABDELIN
Your flattering arts are vain:
Make haste, and execute what I ordain. [To the **GUARDS**.

ALMANZOR
 Cut piece-meal in this cause,
From every wound I should new vigour take,
And every limb should new Almanzors make.

[He puts himself before the **QUEEN**; the **GUARDS** attack him, with the **KING**.

[Enter **ABDELMELECH**.

ABDELMELECH
What angry god, to exercise his spite, [To the **KING**.
Has arm'd your left hand, to cut off your right?

[The **KING** turns, the fight ceases.

The foes are entered at the Elvira gate:
False Lyndaraxa has the town betrayed,
And all the Zegrys give the Spaniards aid.

BOABDELIN
O mischief, not suspected nor foreseen!

ABDELMELECH
Already they have gained the Zacatin,
And thence the Vivarambla place possest,
While our faint soldiers scarce defend the rest.
The duke of Arcos does one squadron head,

The next by Ferdinand himself is led.

ALMANZOR
Now, brave Almanzor, be a god again;
Above our crimes and your own passions reign.
My lord has been by jealousy misled,
To think I was not faithful to his bed.
I can forgive him, though my death he sought,
For too much love can never be a fault.
Protect him, then; and what to his defence
You give not, give to clear my innocence.

ALMANZOR
 Listen, sweet heaven, and all ye blessed above,
Take rules of virtue from a mortal love!
You've raised my soul; and if it mount more high,
'Tis as the wren did on the eagle fly.
Yes, I once more will my revenge neglect,
And, whom you can forgive, I can protect.

BOABDELIN
How hard a fate is mine, still doomed to shame!
I make occasions for my rival's fame!

[Exeunt. An alarm within.

[Enter **FERDINAND, ISABELLA,** Don **ALONZO D'AGUILAR; SPANIARDS** and **LADIES.**

KING FERDINAND
Already more than half the town is gained,
But there is yet a doubtful fight maintained.

ALONZO D'AGUILAR
The fierce young king the entered does attack,
And the more fierce Almanzor drives them back.

KING FERDINAND
The valiant Moors like raging lions fight;
Each youth encouraged by his lady's sight.

QUEEN ISABELLA
I will advance with such a shining train,
That Moorish beauties shall oppose in vain.
Into the press of clashing swords we'll go,
And, where the darts fly thickest, seek the foe.

KING FERDINAND
May heaven, which has inspired this generous thought,

Avert those dangers you have boldly sought!
Call up more troops; the women, to our shame,
Will ravish from the men their part of fame.

[Exeunt **ISABELLA** and **LADIES**.

[Enter **ALABEZ,** and kisses the King's hand.

ALABEZ
 Fair Lyndaraxa, and the Zegry line,
Have led their forces with your troops to join;
The adverse part, which obstinately fought,
Are broke, and Abdelmelech prisoner brought.

KING FERDINAND
Fair Lyndaraxa, and her friends, shall find
The effects of an obliged and grateful mind.

ALABEZ
 But, marching by the Vivarambla place,
The combat carried a more doubtful face.
In that vast square the Moors and Spaniards met,
Where the fierce conflict is continued yet;
But with advantage on the adverse side,
Whom fierce Almanzor does to conquest guide.

KING FERDINAND
With my Castilian foot I'll meet his rage;

[Is going out: Shouts within are heard,—Victoria! Victoria!

[But these loud clamours better news presage.

[Enter the **DUKE OF ARCOS**, and **SOLDIERS**; their Swords drawn and bloody.

DUKE OF ARCOS
Granada now is yours; and there remain
No Moors, but such as own the power of Spain.
That squadron, which their king in person led,
We charged, but found Almanzor on their head:
Three several times we did the Moors attack,
And thrice with slaughter did he drive us back:
Our troops then shrunk; and still we lost more ground,
'Till from our queen we needful succour found:
Her guards to our assistance bravely flew,
And with fresh vigour did the fight renew:
At the same time
Did Lyndaraxa with her troops appear,

And, while we charged the front, engaged the rear:
Then fell the king, slain by a Zegry's hand.

KING FERDINAND

How could he such united force withstand?

DUKE OF ARCOS

Discouraged with his death, the Moorish powers
Fell back, and, falling back, were pressed by ours;
But as, when winds and rain together crowd,
They swell till they have burst the bladdered cloud;
And first the lightning, flashing deadly clear,
Flies, falls, consumes, kills ere it does appear,—
So from his shrinking troops, Almanzor flew,
Each blow gave wounds, and with each wound he slew:
His force at once I envied and admired,
And rushing forward, where my men retired,
Advanced alone.

KING FERDINAND

You hazarded too far
Your person, and the fortune of the war.

DUKE OF ARCOS

Already both our arms for fight did bare,
Already held them threatening in the air,
When heaven (it must be heaven) my sight did guide
To view his arm, upon whose wrist I spied
A ruby cross in diamond bracelets tied;
And just above it, in the brawnier part,
By nature was engraved a bloody heart:
Struck with these tokens, which so well I knew,
And staggering back some paces, I withdrew:
He followed, and supposed it was my fear;
When, from above, a shrill voice reached his ear:—
"Strike not thy father!"—it was heard to cry;
Amazed, and casting round his wondrous eye,
He stopped; then, thinking that his fears were vain,
He lifted up his thundering arm again:
Again the voice withheld him from my death;
"Spare, spare his life," it cried, "who gave thee breath!"
Once more he stopped; then threw his sword away;
"Blessed shade," he said, "I hear thee, I obey
Thy sacred voice;" then, in the sight of all,
He at my feet, I on his neck did fall.

KING FERDINAND

O blessed event!

DUKE OF ARCOS

The Moors no longer fought;
But all their safety by submission sought:
Mean time my son grew faint with loss of blood,
And on his bending sword supported stood;
Yet, with a voice beyond his strength, he cried,
"Lead me to live or die by Almahide."

KING FERDINAND

I am not for his wounds less grieved than you:
For, if what now my soul divines prove true,
This is that son, whom in his infancy
You lost, when by my father forced to fly.

DUKE OF ARCOS

His sister's beauty did my passion move,
(The crime for which I suffered was my love.)
Our marriage known, to sea we took our flight:
There, in a storm, Almanzor first saw light.
On his right arm a bloody heart was graved,
(The mark by which, this day, my life was saved:)
The bracelets and the cross his mother tied
About his wrist, ere she in childbed died.
How we were captives made, when she was dead,
And how Almanzor was in Afric bred,
Some other hour you may at leisure hear,
For see, the queen in triumph does appear.

[Enter **QUEEN ISABELLA, LYNDARAXA, LADIES, MOORS** and **SPANIARDS** mixed as **GUARDS, DELMELECH, ABENAMAR, SELIN,** Prisoners.

KING FERDINAND [embracing **QUEEN ISABELLA**]

All stories which Granada's conquest tell,
Shall celebrate the name of Isabel.
Your ladies too, who, in their country's cause,
Led on the men, shall share in your applause;
And, for your sakes, henceforward I ordain,
No lady's dower shall questioned be in Spain,
Fair Lyndaraxa, for the help she lent,
Shall, under tribute, have this government.

ABDELMELECH

O heaven, that I should live to see this day!

LYNDARAXA

You murmur now, but you shall soon obey.
I knew this empire to my fate was owed;

Heaven held it back as long as e'er it could;
For thee, base wretch, I want a torture yet—[To **ABDELMELECH**.
I'll cage thee; thou shalt be my Bajazet.
I on no pavement but on thee will tread;
And, when I mount, my foot shall know thy head.

ABDELMELECH (Stabbing her with a poniard.)
This first shall know thy heart.

LYNDARAXA
O! I am slain!

ABDELMELECH
Now, boast thy country is betrayed to Spain.

KING FERDINAND
Look to the lady!—Seize the murderer!

ABDELMELECH [Stabbing himself.]
I do myself that justice I did her.
Thy blood I to thy ruined country give,
[To **LYNDARAXA**.
But love too well thy murder to out-live.
Forgive a love, excused by its excess,
Which, had it not been cruel, had been less.
Condemn my passion, then, but pardon me,
And think I murdered him who murdered thee.

[Dies.

LYNDARAXA
Die for us both; I have not leisure now;
A crown is come, and will not fate allow:
And yet I feel something like death is near,
My guards, my guards,—
Let not that ugly skeleton appear!
Sure destiny mistakes; this death's not mine;
She dotes, and meant to cut another line.
Tell her I am a queen;—but 'tis too late;
Dying, I charge rebellion on my fate.
Bow down, ye slaves:—[To the MOORS.
Bow quickly down, and your submission show.—

[They bow.

I'm pleased to taste an empire ere I go.

[Dies.

SELIN

She's dead, and here her proud ambition ends.

ABENAMAR

Such fortune still such black designs attends.

KING FERDINAND

Remove those mournful objects from our eyes,
And see performed their funeral obsequies.

[The bodies are carried off.

[Enter **ALMANZOR** and **ALMAHIDE**, **OZMYN** and **BENZAYDA**; **ALMAHIDE** brought in a chair; **ALMANZOR**
led betwixt **SOLDIERS**. **ISABELLA** salutes **ALMAHIDE** in dumb show.

DUKE OF ARCOS (Presenting **ALMANZOR** to the **KING**.)

See here that son, whom I with pride call mine;
And who dishonours not your royal line.

KING FERDINAND

I'm now secure, this sceptre, which I gain,
Shall be continued in the power of Spain;
Since he, who could alone my foes defend,
By birth and honour is become my friend;
Yet I can own no joy, nor conquest boast, [To **ALMANZOR**.
While in this blood I see how dear it cost.

ALMANZOR

This honour to my veins new blood will bring;
Streams cannot fail, fed by so high a spring.
But all court-customs I so little know,
That I may fail in those respects I owe.
I bring a heart which homage never knew;
Yet it finds something of itself in you:
Something so kingly, that my haughty mind
Is drawn to yours, because 'tis of a kind.

QUEEN ISABELLA

And yet that soul, which bears itself so high,
If fame be true, admits a sovereignty.
This queen, in her fair eyes, such fetters brings,
As chain that heart, which scorns the power of kings.

ALMAHIDE

Little of charm in these sad eyes appears;
If they had any, now 'tis lost in tears.
A crown, and husband, ravished in one day!—

Excuse a grief, I cannot choose but pay.

QUEEN ISABELLA
Have courage, madam; heaven has joys in store,
To recompence those losses you deplore.

ALMAHIDE
I know your God can all my woes redress;
To him I made my vows in my distress:
And, what a misbeliever vowed this day,
Though not a queen, a Christian yet shall pay.

QUEEN ISABELLA (Embracing her.)
That Christian name you shall receive from me,
And Isabella of Granada be.

BENZAYDA
This blessed change we all with joy receive;
And beg to learn that faith which you believe.

QUEEN ISABELLA
With reverence for those holy rites prepare;
And all commit your fortunes to my care.

KING FERDINAND [to **ALMAHIDE**]
You, madam, by that crown you lose, may gain,
If you accept, a coronet of Spain,
Of which Almanzor's father stands possest.

QUEEN ISABELLA [to **ALMAHIDE**]
May you in him, and he in you, be blest!

ALMAHIDE
I owe my life and honour to his sword;
But owe my love to my departed lord.

ALMANZOR
Thus, when I have no living force to dread,
Fate finds me enemies amongst the dead.
I'm now to conquer ghosts, and to destroy
The strong impressions of a bridal joy.

ALMAHIDE
You've yet a greater foe than these can be,—
Virtue opposes you, and modesty.

ALMANZOR
From a false fear that modesty does grow,

And thinks true love, because 'tis fierce, its foe.
'Tis but the wax whose seals on virgins stay:
Let it approach love's fire, 'twill melt away:—
But I have lived too long; I never knew,
When fate was conquered, I must combat you.
I thought to climb the steep ascent of love;
But did not think to find a foe above.
'Tis time to die, when you my bar must be,
Whose aid alone could give me victory;
Without,
I'll pull up all the sluices of the flood,
And love, within, shall boil out all my blood.

QUEEN ISABELLA
Fear not your love should find so sad success,
While I have power to be your patroness.
I am her parent now, and may command
So much of duty as to give her hand.

[Gives him **ALMAHIDE'S** hand.

ALMAHIDE
Madam, I never can dispute your power,
Or as a parent, or a conqueror;
But, when my year of widowhood expires,
Shall yield to your command, and his desires.

ALMANZOR
 Move swiftly, sun, and fly a lover's pace;
Leave weeks and months behind thee in thy race!

KING FERDINAND
Mean time, you shall my victories pursue,
The Moors in woods and mountains to subdue.

ALMANZOR
 The toils of war shall help to wear each day,
And dreams of love shall drive my nights away.—
Our banners to the Alhambra's turrets bear;
Then, wave our conquering crosses in the air,
And cry, with shouts of triumph,—Live and reign,
Great Ferdinand and Isabel of Spain!

[Exeunt.

EPILOGUE

They, who have best succeeded on the stage,
Have still conformed their genius to their age.
Thus Jonson did mechanic humour show,
When men were dull, and conversation low.
Then comedy was faultless, but 'twas coarse:
Cobb's tankard was a jest, and Otter's horse[1].
And, as their comedy, their love was mean;
Except, by chance, in some one laboured scene,
Which must atone for an ill-written play.
They rose, but at their height could seldom stay.
Fame then was cheap, and the first comer sped;
And they have kept it since, by being dead.
But, were they now to write, when critics weigh
Each line, and every word, throughout a play,
None of them, no not Jonson in his height,
Could pass, without allowing grains for weight.
Think it not envy, that these truths are told;
Our poet's not malicious, though he's bold.
'Tis not to brand them, that their faults are shown,
But, by their errors, to excuse his own.
If love and honour now are higher raised,
'Tis not the poet, but the age is praised.
Wit's now arrived to a more high degree;
Our native language more refined and free.
Our ladies and our men now speak more wit
In conversation, than those poets writ.
Then, one of these is, consequently, true;
That what this poet writes comes short of you,
And imitates you ill (which most he fears),
Or else his writing is not worse than theirs.
Yet, though you judge (as sure the critics will),
That some before him writ with greater skill,
In this one praise he has their fame surpast,
To please an age more gallant than the last.

Footnote

1. The characters alluded to are Cobb, the water bearer, in "Every Man in his Humour;" and Captain Otter, in "Epicene, or the Silent Woman," whose humour it was to christen his drinking cups by the names of Horse, Bull, and Bear.]

John Dryden – A Short Biography

John Dryden was born on August 9th, 1631 in the village rectory of Aldwincle near Thrapston in Northamptonshire, where his maternal grandfather was Rector of All Saints Church.

Dryden was the eldest of fourteen children born to Erasmus Dryden and wife Mary Pickering, paternal grandson of Sir Erasmus Dryden, 1st Baronet (1553–1632) and wife Frances Wilkes, Puritan landowning gentry who supported the Puritan cause and Parliament.

As a boy Dryden lived in the nearby village of Titchmarsh, Northamptonshire where it is probable that he received his first education.

In 1644 he was sent to Westminster School as a King's Scholar where his headmaster was Dr. Richard Busby, a charismatic teacher but severe disciplinarian. Having recently been re-founded by Elizabeth I, Westminster now embraced a very different religious and political spirit encouraging royalism and high Anglicanism but as a humanist public school, it maintained a curriculum which trained pupils in the art of rhetoric and the presentation of arguments for both sides of a given issue. This skill would remain with Dryden and influence his later writing and thinking, as much of it displays these dialectical patterns.

His first published poem, whilst still at Westminster, was an elegy with a strong royalist flavour on the death of his schoolmate Henry, Lord Hastings from smallpox, and alludes to the execution of King Charles I, which took place on January 30th, 1649.

In 1650 Dryden was ready for University and travelled to Trinity College, Cambridge. Dryden's undergraduate years would almost certainly have followed the standard curriculum of classics, rhetoric, and mathematics.

Dryden obtained his BA in 1654, graduating top of the list for Trinity that year.

However family tragedy struck in June of the same year when Dryden's father died, leaving him some land which generated a small income, but not enough to live on.

Returning to London during The Protectorate, Dryden now obtained work with Cromwell's Secretary of State, John Thurloe. This may have been the result of influence exercised on his behalf by his cousin the Lord Chamberlain, Sir Gilbert Pickering.

At Cromwell's funeral on 23 November 1658 Dryden was in the company of the Puritan poets John Milton and Andrew Marvell. The setting was to be a sea change in English history. From Republic to Monarchy and from one set of lauded poets to what would soon become the Age of Dryden.

The start began later that year when Dryden published the first of his great poems, Heroic Stanzas (1658), a eulogy on Cromwell's death which is necessarily cautious and prudent in its emotional display.

With the Restoration of the Monarchy in 1660 Dryden celebrated in verse with Astraea Redux, an authentic royalist panegyric. In this work the interregnum is illustrated as a time of anarchy, and Charles is seen as the restorer of peace and order.

With the king now established Dryden moved quickly to place himself as the leading poet and critic of his day and transferred his allegiances to the new government.

Along with Astraea Redux, Dryden welcomed the new regime with two more panegyrics: To His Sacred Majesty: A Panegyric on his Coronation (1662) and To My Lord Chancellor (1662).

These panegyrics are occasional and written to celebrate events. Thus they are written for the nation rather than the self, but these and others put him in good standing for his eventual appointment as Poet Laureate, where a number of event poems would be required each year and speaking for the Nation and to the Nation would be the first order of duty.

These poems suggest that Dryden was looking to court a possible patron which would have given him an income and time to explore his creative ideas but no, his path instead would be to make a living in writing for publishers, not for the aristocracy, and thus ultimately for the reading public.

In November 1662 Dryden was proposed for membership in the Royal Society, and he was elected an early fellow. However, his inactivity and non payment of dues led to his expulsion in 1666.

On December 1st, 1663 Dryden married the Royalist sister of Sir Robert Howard—Lady Elizabeth Howard (died 1714). The marriage was at St. Swithin's, London, and the consent of the parents is noted on the license, though Lady Elizabeth was then about twenty-five. She was the object of some scandals, well or ill founded; it was said that Dryden had been bullied into the marriage by her brothers. A small estate in Wiltshire was settled upon them by her father. The lady's intellect and temper were apparently not good; her husband was treated as an inferior by those of her social status.

Dryden's works occasionally contain outbursts against the married state but also celebrations of the same. Little else is known of the intimate side of his marriage.

Both Dryden and his wife were warmly attached to their children. They had three sons: Charles (1666–1704), John (1668–1701), and Erasmus Henry (1669–1710). Lady Elizabeth Dryden survived her husband, but went insane soon after his death and died in 1714.

With the re-opening of the theatres after the Puritan ban, Dryden began to also write plays. His first play, The Wild Gallant, appeared in 1663 but was not successful. From 1668 on he was contracted to produce three plays a year for the King's Company, in which he became a shareholder. During the 1660s and '70s, theatrical writing was his main source of income. He led the way in Restoration comedy, his best-known works being Marriage à la Mode (1672), as well as heroic tragedy and regular tragedy, in which his greatest success was All for Love (1678). Dryden was never fully satisfied with his theatrical writings and frequently suggested that his talents were wasted on unworthy audiences.

Certainly therefore fame as a poet looked more rewarding. In 1667, around the same time his dramatic career began, he published Annus Mirabilis, a lengthy historical poem which described the English defeat of the Dutch naval fleet and the Great Fire of London in 1666. It was a modern epic in pentameter quatrains that established him as the pre-eminent poet of his generation, and was crucial in his attaining the posts of Poet Laureate (1668) and then historiographer royal (1670).

When the Great Plague of London closed the theatres in 1665 Dryden retreated to Wiltshire where he wrote Of Dramatick Poesie (1668), arguably the best of his unsystematic prefaces and essays. Dryden constantly defended his own literary practice, and Of Dramatick Poesie, the longest of his critical works, takes the form of a dialogue in which four characters—each based on a prominent contemporary, with Dryden himself as 'Neander'—debate the merits of classical, French and English drama.

He felt strongly about the relation of the poet to tradition and the creative process, and his heroic play Aureng-zebe (1675) has a prologue which denounces the use of rhyme in serious drama. His play All for Love (1678) was written in blank verse, and was to immediately follow Aureng-Zebe.

On December 18th, 1679 he was attacked in Rose Alley near his home in Covent Garden by thugs hired by fellow poet, John Wilmot, 2nd Earl of Rochester, with whom he had a long-standing conflict. Wilmot was constantly in and out of favour with the King and his own poetry was often bawdy, lewd, even obscene and made fun of the King who would often exile him from Court.

Dryden's greatest achievements were in satiric verse: the mock-heroic Mac Flecknoe, a more personal product of his Laureate years, was a lampoon circulated in manuscript and an attack on the playwright Thomas Shadwell. Dryden's main goal in the work is to "satirize Shadwell, ostensibly for his offenses against literature but more immediately we may suppose for his habitual badgering of him on the stage and in print." It is not a belittling form of satire, but rather one which makes his object great in ways which are unexpected, transferring the ridiculous into poetry. This line of satire continued with Absalom and Achitophel (1681) and The Medal (1682). Other major works from this period are the religious poems Religio Laici (1682), written from the position of a member of the Church of England; his 1683 edition of Plutarch's Lives, translated From the Greek by Several Hands in which he introduced the word biography to English readers; and The Hind and the Panther, (1687) which celebrates his conversion to Roman Catholicism.

He wrote Britannia Rediviva celebrating the birth of a son and heir to the Catholic King and Queen on June 10th, 1688. When later in the same year James II was deposed in the Glorious Revolution, Dryden's refusal to take the oaths of allegiance to the new monarchs, William and Mary, which left him out of favour at court and he had to leave his post as Poet Laureate. Thomas Shadwell, his despised rival, succeeded him. Dryden, England's greatest literary figure, was now forced to give up his public offices and live by the proceeds of his pen alone.

Dryden was an excellent translator with his own style which brought the ire of many critics. Many felt he would embellish or expand anything he felt short or curt. Dryden did not feel such expansion was a fault, arguing that as Latin is a naturally concise language it cannot be duly represented by a comparable number of words in the much larger English vocabulary. He continued with his task of translating works by Horace, Juvenal, Ovid, Lucretius, and Theocritus, a task which he found far more satisfying than writing for the stage.

In 1694 he began work on what would be his most ambitious and defining work as translator, The Works of Virgil (1697), which was published by subscription. The publication of the translation of Virgil was a national event and brought Dryden the sum of £1,400.

His final translations appeared in the volume Fables Ancient and Modern (1700), a series of episodes from Homer, Ovid, and Boccaccio, as well as modernised adaptations from Geoffrey Chaucer interspersed with Dryden's own poems. As a translator, he made great literary works in the older languages available to readers of English.

John Dryden died on May 12th, 1700, and was initially buried in St. Anne's cemetery in Soho, before being exhumed and reburied in Westminster Abbey ten days later. He was the subject of poetic eulogies, such as Luctus Brittannici: or the Tears of the British Muses; for the Death of John Dryden, Esq. (London, 1700), and The Nine Muses.

He is seen as dominating the literary life of Restoration England to such a point that the period came to be known in literary circles as the Age of Dryden. Walter Scott called him "Glorious John."

Dryden was the dominant literary figure and influence of his age. He established the heroic couplet as a standard form of English poetry by writing successful satires, religious pieces, fables, epigrams, compliments, prologues, and plays with it; he also introduced the alexandrine and triplet into the form. In his poems, translations, and criticism, he established a poetic diction appropriate to the heroic couplet—Auden referred to him as "the master of the middle style"—that was a model for his contemporaries and for much of the 18th century. The considerable loss felt by the English literary community at his death was evident in the elegies written about him. Dryden's heroic couplet went on to become the dominant poetic form of the 18th century.

What Dryden achieved in his poetry was neither the emotional excitement of the early nineteenth-century romantics nor the intellectual complexities of the metaphysicals. Although he uses formal structures such as heroic couplets, he tried to recreate the natural rhythm of speech, and he knew that different subjects need different kinds of verse. In his preface to Religio Laici he says that "the expressions of a poem designed purely for instruction ought to be plain and natural, yet majestic... The florid, elevated and figurative way is for the passions; for (these) are begotten in the soul by showing the objects out of their true proportion.... A man is to be cheated into passion, but to be reasoned into truth."

Perhaps the following illustrates Dryden and his life—"The way I have taken, is not so streight as Metaphrase, nor so loose as Paraphrase: Some things too I have omitted, and sometimes added of my own. Yet the omissions I hope, are but of Circumstances, and such as wou'd have no grace in English; and the Addition, I also hope, are easily deduc'd from Virgil's Sense. They will seem (at least I have the Vanity to think so), not struck into him, but growing out of him".

John Dryden – A Concise Bibliography

Astraea Redux, 1660
The Wild Gallant (comedy), 1663
The Indian Emperour (tragedy), 1665
Annus Mirabilis (poem), 1667
The Enchanted Island (comedy), 1667, with William D'Avenant from Shakespeare's The Tempest
Secret Love, or The Maiden Queen, 1667
An Essay of Dramatick Poesie, 1668
An Evening's Love (comedy), 1668
Tyrannick Love (tragedy), 1669
The Conquest of Granada, 1670
The Assignation, or Love in a Nunnery, 1672
Marriage à la mode, 1672
Amboyna, or the Cruelties of the Dutch to the English Merchants, 1673
The Mistaken Husband (comedy), 1674
Aureng-zebe, 1675
All for Love, 1678

Oedipus (heroic drama), 1679, an adaptation with Nathaniel Lee of Sophocles' Oedipus
Absalom and Achitophel, 1681
The Spanish Fryar, 1681
Mac Flecknoe, 1682
The Medal, 1682
Religio Laici, 1682
To the Memory of Mr. Oldham, 1684
Threnodia Augustalis, 1685
The Hind and the Panther, 1687
A Song for St. Cecilia's Day, 1687
Britannia Rediviva, 1688, written to mark the birth of a Prince of Wales.
Amphitryon, 1690
Don Sebastian (play), 1690
Creator Spirit, by whose aid, 1690. Translation of Rabanus Maurus' Veni Creator Spiritus
King Arthur, 1691
Cleomenes, 1692
The Art of Satire, 1693
Love Triumphant, 1694
The Works of Virgil, 1697
Alexander's Feast, 1697
Fables, Ancient and Modern, 1700

www.ingramcontent.com/pod-product-compliance
Lightning Source LLC
Chambersburg PA
CBHW060130050426
42448CB00010B/2058